CLIL

Discuss the Changing World

Miyako Nakaya   Miyuki Yukita
Masaru Yamazaki   Chad L. Godfrey

SEIBIDO

音声ファイルのダウンロード／ストリーミング

CD マーク表示がある箇所は、音声を弊社 HP より無料でダウンロード／ストリーミングすることができます。トップページのバナーをクリックし、書籍検索してください。書籍詳細ページに音声ダウンロードアイコンがございますのでそちらから自習用音声としてご活用ください。

https://www.seibido.co.jp

CLIL : Discuss the Changing World

は　し　が　き

　学生のみなさんは、英語のディスカッションで発言することは得意ですか、苦手ですか？　苦手だという方のほうが圧倒的に多いのではないでしょうか？　それは単純に人の前で話すのは苦手とか、自分の意見はとるに足らないものだとか、自分の意見を友達がどう思うか心配だとか、学習とは関係のない心理的な要素が大きいかもしれません。

　その上に、英語の問題も大きいと思います。表現がわからず自分の言いたいことが言えないという状況では、伝えることをあきらめてしまう方も多いかもしれません。また、そもそもトピック自体、知識がないとか興味がないから意見も持てないということがあるかもしれません。さらに、ディスカッションを進めるときのルールなども知らないと、自分の意見を1回発言したあとはどうすればよいのかわからなかったり、また、自分の意見と違う人がいても反論する気が引けてしまったりします。そんなときは、ディスカッション中もただうなずいていることになりがちです。

　このような山積みの問題をひとつずつ解決していこうというのがこのテキストです。Content and Language Integrated Learning(CLIL) のアプローチを使い、formal discussion ができるようになるというゴールに向かって、内容と言語を同時に学んでいけるように構成されています。1ユニットごとに、新しいトピックの語彙・表現、内容についての情報、話し合いのルールやマナー、論理的思考・展開、結論の導き方など、さまざまなことを学べるように作られています。これをユニットごとに何度も繰り返し学習することで、さまざまなトピックの情報を得て、英語表現を学習しながら、自分の意見を形成しそれを伝えることに慣れていくことができます。

　トピックの内容はAI、その他のテクノロジーの発達で、急速に私たちの生活や価値観が変わっていく状況を切り取ったものです。学生のみなさんが自分で体験していることです。自分には関係ないということはないはずです。それらの情報を英語で得て、少しでも英語で発信できる力を身につければ、世界も広がり、自信もつくはずです。内容を楽しみながら、ぜひ他の人に自分の考えを発信し、話し合う力をつけてください。

　学生のみなさんの明るい未来に、少しでもお役に立てることができればうれしいです。

　出版にあたっては、田村栄一氏をはじめ、皆様から貴重なご助言をいただきました。心からお礼を申し上げます。

2019 年 10 月

著者一同

CONTENTS

以下のトピックを例にして、学習のステップを説明します。

Topic: Healthy Food-Bananas

Introduction

A Listening

トピックに関してのニュースを聞きます。空欄には、数字、トピックのキーワード、一般的な重要語句、聞き取りにくい語彙などが入ります。ここでまず、これから扱うトピックに慣れていきます。

B key phrases

前のリスニングやこれから出てくるリーディングなど、トピックについての話をするときに役に立つフレーズの意味を辞書で調べて日本語で確認します。

C Three picture

3 つの絵についてペアで話し合います。

1.

2.
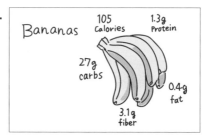

3.

1. There are three bananas. / I can see a bunch of bananas. / They are yellow. It looks delicious.

2. Picture 2 shows nutrients of bananas. A banana contains 1.3 g of protein. / Bananas has 105 calories.

3. There are some pieces of bananas on the top of cornflakes in a bowl. / The cornflakes are brown, so it might be chocolate taste. It is served with orange juice, so this picture is probably breakfast.

▶**クラスのレベルに応じて青文字の文型で示されているような英文を 2 つぐらいペアで言ってみましょう。**

Reading

300 語前後の読み物を通してさらにトピックの内容を掘り下げます。これらの情報は、のちに自分の意見を構築するときのエビデンスやそのヒントになります。

A questions

リーディングの内容についての理解を確認します。

B outline

アウトラインの穴埋めをします。全体の構成を確認することで、内容についての理解をさらに深めます。

アウトラインの形	だいたいパラグラフごとにひとつのトピックを見つけます。アウトラインの形は次のようになっています。

1. トピック
　　A. その下にあるサポートアイディア
　　　　1. 細かい例や説明
　　　　　　a. さらに細かい例や説明

新しいトピックや説明の見つけ方	新しいパラグラフ、または、first, second, finally や , However, Moreover, Recently などのつなぎ言葉が目印になります。

Data

A トピックに関連したグラフや表などを見て、より深く、トピックの理解に努めます。図の下には、それぞれの説明文があります。その中の空欄に答えを書き込みながら、図やグラフの読み方を学び、同時に内容について理解をします。

B さらにもう一つ、図やグラフなどを見ながら会話文を完成させ、内容の理解を深めます。この会話文に触れることで、次のディスカッションの例や見本にもなります。

▶**ここまでのリスニング、リーディング、データに含まれていた情報と語彙・表現、そしてポイントを、この後のディスカッションで大いに活用してください。**

Step 1. まず、命題についての自分が賛成か反対かを選び、その後に2つか3つの理由を書きます。さらに自分とは逆の意見も考え、2つか3つの理由を書きます。次に、ペアでどんな意見や理由が出たか比較して、意見を出し合います。それにより、Critical thinking と英語表現の練習をします。

Step 2. 1. 2つの会話例を、論点を考えながらパートナーと読み合い、どのような英語の表現が使われているか、会話例をディスカッション・ストラテジーに合わせて分類します。

2. 次にエビデンスを探します。エビデンスとは、外部ソースからの具体的な例や、研究した結果の数字、アンケートの結果、あるいは専門家の意見などのことです。

▶ エビデンスの意味　解説参照

▶ エビデンスの文献を探すときのコツ　解説参照

Step 3. パートナーと相反する立場に立ち、下記のようなディスカッションのダイアログを作ります。初めは、2往復をめざします。

ダイアログの作り方

Statement	We should eat bananas every day.		
Presenters	Mr. Sato and Ms. Shio	Date	April 14, 2019
Dialogue			
Mr. Sato	I agree with this idea because bananas are nutritious.		
	Evidence: According to the George Mateljan Foundation, bananas are the world's healthiest food.		
	Source: The George Mateljan Foundation (2015) http://www.whfoods.com/genpage.php?tname=foodspice&dbid=7 (retrieved April 15, 2019)		
Ms. Shio	That is true. Bananas are high in calories. So, if people eat them every day, they will gain weight. That's why I disagree with this idea.		
	Evidence: COCOKARA reports that they contain a lot of carbohydrates, mainly sugars in ripe bananas. Consuming too many may lead to an increase in weight, which increases the risk of developing diabetes.		
	Source:COCOKARA https://cocokara-next.com/food_and_diet/intake-of-fruit-02-tt/ (retrieved April 17 2019)		
Mr. Sato	You have a point. However, bananas contain important nutrients.		

Step 4. 全体のダイアログをもう1度パートナーと読み合います。

Step 5. 次にディスカッションの結論を考えます。Step 4までは、パートナーと相反する立場に立って対話してきましたが、ここからは、対話の結果、意見が変わることもあるでしょう。もし、パートナーと同じ意見になったら、1つの結論を書き、そうでない場合は、双方の意見を書きます。さらに、クラスで他のペアがどのような結論に達したかを発表すれば、お互いに学ぶことができます。

結論の伝え方

●ひとつの結論に達したとき（賛成）
We reached the same conclusion. Both of us agree that we should eat bananas every day mainly because bananas have been proved to be one of the world's healthiest foods. Therefore, we should eat them every day.

●ひとつの結論に達したとき（反対）
We reached the same conclusion. Both of us disagree that we should eat bananas every day. Although bananas may be highly nutritious, eating them every day may increase our risk of developing diabetes. Therefore, we shouldn't eat them every day.

●ひとつの結論に達しなかったとき
We didn't reach the same conclusion. One of us agrees that we should eat bananas every day mainly because bananas are highly nutritious, and the other disagrees with it mainly because eating them every day may lead to diabetes.

Step 6. 同じトピックで、ずっとパートナーだった相手と離れて、新しい4人のグループを作りグループディスカッションをします。エビデンスは賛成・反対両方もっているはずなので、話し合いでも、じゃんけんでも、2人ずつ同じサイドになって議論します。

▶ 「ディスカッションの基本ルール」解説参照

▶ 「ディスカッションの進め方」解説参照

最後に、各自、もっと知りたいことについてトピックを決め、リサーチをし、それを発表したり、レポートにまとめたりします。これで、ディスカッションのトピックについての知識や考えがさらに深まります。また、プレゼンテーションやライティングのスキルも伸ばします。

解説

エビデンスの意味

フォーマルなディスカッションにおいては、自分の考えを述べるだけではなく、それをサポートする証拠が必要になります。これにより説得力が増します。

エビデンスの文献を探すときのコツ

探し方はさまざまです。インターネットで検索したり、本を読んだり、新聞や雑誌を読んだり、ニュースで見たりしたことがエビデンスになります。この時に重要なのは、情報源をしっかりと記録して、ディスカッションのときに提示することです。また、インターネットから情報は、それを見た日付も控えておきます。情報源はより信頼のおけるものが望ましいです。説得力が増すからです。企業や団体、公的機関、専門家などが公的に発信しているものは、より信頼性が高いと言えるでしょう。個人のブログはできるだけ避けますが、それが専門家のものであれば、より説得力があるかもしれません。自分自身で、その情報がどれくらい信頼性があるかを客観的に判断し、ディスカッションで自分の意見をサポートしましょう。

ディスカッションの基本ルール

1. ディスカッションの目的を理解する：（一般的なディスカッションの場合）
   賛成と反対の意見交換だけが目的なのか？
   グループとしての結論を出すことなのか？
   解決策を考えることなのか？

   このテキストでは、賛成と反対の意見交換と、もし結論が一致すればその結論を出す。一致しなければ、そのまま主張し合う。

2. 一人の発言者ばかり発言したり、長く話をしたりしない。

3. 自分の前に発言者がいる場合は、よくその内容を聞き、自分とは反対の意見でも好意的な言葉を述べてから、自分の発言をする。

   例): That's a good point, but… / You have a good point, but …/

4. 相手の発言がわからない、聞こえない場合は、質問をして確認する。

ディスカッションの進め方

ディスカッションは司会が進行します。二人のディスカッションでもグループのディスカッションでも、ひとりは、司会者（Facilitator）を兼ねます。司会者は次のようなフレーズを使い、話し合いを進めていきます。

司会進行のやり方

表現 1. Today, we will discuss whether we should eat bananas every day for our health.

表現 2. Today's topic is whether we should eat bananas every day for our health.

このあとに、決まりごとではありませんが、まず、司会者が自分の意見を簡単に述べて始めると、話し合いがスムーズに始まります。

例): I think we should eat bananas, but not every day because We might gain our weight. So, I disagree with this idea.
Mr. Koba, what do you think about today's topic?

このあとも、司会者はどんどん参加者の発言を求めます。二人の場合は、交互に話すということが基本になります。

表現 1. How about this point? Do you agree with Mr. Koba's idea?

表現 2. Is there anyone who would like to say more?

表現 3. Who has another point of view?

最後にまとめに入ります。

全員同意の場合

表現 1. We reached the same conclusion. Both of us (We) agree with the statement mainly because bananas are good for our health.

表現 2. We all agree that we should eat bananas every day because it is good for our health.

全員同意しなかった場合

表現 1. We did not reach the same conclusion. One (some of us) agrees with the statement mainly because bananas are good for our health, but the other (others) disagrees with this statement mainly because eating bananas every day is too much calories and too much sugar.

It seems that bananas are healthy food. However, eating them every day is controversial. I hope that each one of us will find an appropriate way to eat them.

最後に締めくくりの言葉を述べます。

表現 1. This is all the time we have for today. / That's all for today.

表現 2. Thank you for your cooperation. / Thank you for your participation.

UNIT 1

Artificial Intelligence: How Will Humans Live with AI?

Introduction

1-02

A Listen to the following news story and fill in the blanks.

An English-language tourism ¹(   ), The Japan Trip Navigator, was released in 2018. It was created by Microsoft Japan in partnership with two Japanese companies, JTB and NAVITIME. On the application, tourists from ²(   ) can see more than 100 model ³(   ) plans offered by JTB, which can help them to plan their own trips. Tourists can ask ⁴(   ) ⁵ about sightseeing spots, and an ⁵(   ) tourist guide, Miko, answers them. Miko is an AI-powered chatbot developed by Microsoft. Miko will become ⁶(   ) as more people use it. What is more, with the help of a navigation ⁷(   ) offered by NAVITIME, tourists will not lose their way.

B The following are key phrases for the topic. Look them up in your dictionary and write the meanings.

1. artificial intelligence   _____
2. personalize the data   _____
3. predictive search   _____
4. the history of past searches   _____
5. analyze account information   _____
6. diagnose diseases   _____
7. the Technological Singularity   _____

C What do you see in these pictures? Talk about it with your partner.

1.

2.

3.

Artificial intelligence (AI) is the ability of a machine to imitate human intelligence, including factors such as reasoning, learning and self-improvement. Anyone who has ever used a search engine such as Google has interacted with AI. First, the AI behind a search engine acquires information about someone and
5 learns patterns of the user. Then by using these patterns, it personalizes the data and reaches conclusions. For example, Google's predictive search uses AI. The machine learns from the history of the user's past searches and it predicts what the user will be typing in the search box. Online retailers also use AI to gather information about the customer's preferences and buying habits. They personalize his or her shopping
10 experience and suggest new products that the customer may like.

AI is used in various industries. For example, many banks now use AI to protect their customers from crimes. The machine analyzes the customers' account information. If it detects unusual transactions, it warns the account holder. AI is also used for commercial airline flights. According to a survey in 2015, Boeing 777
15 pilots spent only seven minutes manually flying the plane. The rest of the flight was conducted by AI. Moreover, more AI technologies will be used in hospitals. AI can help doctors and nurses with their work. It can diagnose diseases faster and more cheaply than humans and drugs will be developed faster at lower prices.

The Technological Singularity is a hypothetical future point when artificial
20 intelligence will surpass human capabilities. An American futurist, Ray Kurzweil, expects the singularity to occur by 2045. He suggests that AI will be so smart that it will come up with ideas that humans cannot even comprehend, and this brilliant AI could solve our problems. By contrast, theoretical physicist, Stephen Hawking had a different idea. He said that humans, who are limited by slow biological evolution,
25 would not be able to compete and would be replaced by AI. Experts have different views about this idea and it is currently a controversial issue.

A Read the passage and answer the questions.

1. What kinds of processes can AI do?

_____

2. How will AI be used in hospitals?

_____

3. What is the Technological Singularity?

_____

B Complete an outline of the reading passage.

I. Artificial intelligence

    A. How it works

        1. The machine acquires _____.

        2. The machine learns _____ and uses them.

        3. The machine _____ the data.

        4. The machine reaches _____.

    B. Examples

        1. Google's _____ predicts a user's search terms.

        2. Online retailers use AI to _____ about the customer.

II. AI in industry

    A. Banks

        1. AI _____ customers from crimes.

        2. AI analyzes _____.

        3. AI _____ account holders.

    B. Commercial airline flights

        1. Pilots _____ flew the plane only for seven minutes.

        2. The rest of the flight was conducted by _____.

    C. Hospitals

        1. AI can _____ diseases faster and more cheaply.

        2. AI will make _____ faster at lower prices.

III. The Technological Singularity

    A. The singularity hypothesis

        1. AI will _____ human capabilities.

        2. It may occur _____.

    B. After the singularity

        1. AI could _____ our problems.

        2. AI would _____ humans.

Data

A Study the figure and fill in the blanks.

 1-06

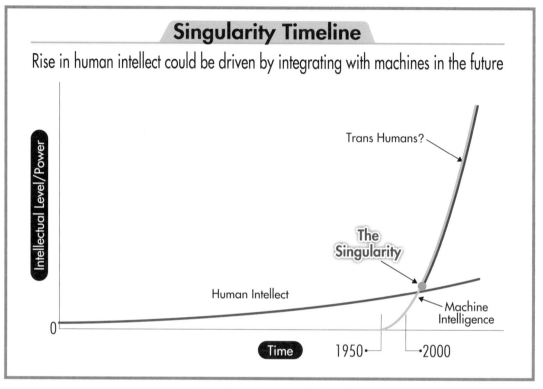

Figure 1: Technological Singularity

Source: Kurzweil, Ray 2006 The Singularity Is Near: When Humans Transcend Biology
https://www.researchgate.net/figure/Technological-Singularity-Source-Kurzweil-2006_fig1_317916895

Figure 1 is a graphical representation of [1]( ) ( ) hypothesis. In this line graph, you see two lines. The red line shows [2]( ) ( ), which has been rising [3]( ). The green line shows [4]( ) ( ). Its history started in [5]( ). Since then, there has been a rapid [6]( ). The point where the two lines meet shows when the [7]( ) will occur. At that point, machine intelligence will reach the level of human intellect. The singularity is expected to occur by 2045. After the singularity, the green line will still continue [8]( ) sharply. Technology will surpass human capabilities and it will expand human intelligence.

NOTES

hypothesis 仮説　intellect 知性

16

B Study the figure and fill in the blanks.

 1-07

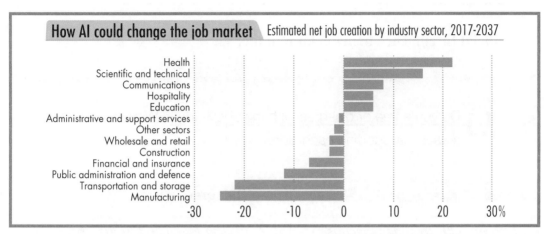

Figure 2: Estimated net job creation by industry sector (2017-2037)

https://www.bbc.com/news/business-44849492
Source: PwC "How AI could change the job market"

A: Experts say AI will create as many jobs as it will displace over the next 20 years.

B: Does this mean some jobs will be created and other jobs will disappear?

A: That's right. Figure 2 shows which sectors would benefit.

B: It looks like there will be increases in health.

A: Yes, jobs in the [1](   ) sector will increase by 22 percent, the 5 [2](   ) (   ) (   ) sector by 16 percent, and in education, there's a 6 percent increase.

B: In contrast, there are many jobs which could fall.

A: That's true. [3](   ) jobs could fall by 25 percent, and transportation and storage by 22 percent. The analysis shows there will be 10 winners and losers.

B: I see. Why do you think the [4](   ) sector will be a winner?

A: More AI will be used in hospitals, so the sector will need people to administer it.

B: How about the [5](   ) sector?

A: In that sector, a good relationship between teachers and students is important, 15 and such jobs won't easily be replaced by machines.

B: I agree. Then why will the [6](   ) sector be a loser?

A: Much of the work in factories can be automated, and so the sector will need fewer workers.

NOTES

displace 〜に取って代わる   analysis 分析   administer 〜を管理する

Discussion

Artificial Intelligence benefits human life.

Step 1. Do you agree or disagree with the above idea? Write two or three reasons supporting each side.

Agree

I agree with this idea because of the following reasons.

✓ **Reason 1**

....
....
....
....

✓ **Reason 2**

....
....
....
....

✓ **Reason 3**

....
....
....
....

Disagree

I disagree with this idea because of the following reasons.

✓ **Reason 1**

....
....
....
....

✓ **Reason 2**

....
....
....
....

✓ **Reason 3**

....
....
....
....

Step 2. Learn the discussion strategies. 1-08、09

1. In pairs, read out the following conversation. Write the numbers of the underlined expressions in the appropriate discussion strategies below.

Referring to a source ____   Starting a discussion ____

Agreeing ____   Asking for an opinion ____

Giving your opinion ____   Disagreeing ____

• *Example 1:*

A: ❶<u>Today we are going to discuss</u> artificial intelligence.

B: ❷<u>I totally agree with using artificial intelligence</u>. More AI technology will be used in hospitals and it will help doctors diagnose diseases.

A: You're right. I heard that AI will make drug development faster and more lives will be saved.

• *Example 2:*

A: Today's topic is artificial intelligence. ❸<u>What's your opinion</u>?

B: I agree because it makes our life more convenient.

A: ❹<u>Maybe, but</u> ❺<u>I think</u> it's not always true. When AI becomes smarter than humans, it may redesign itself and harm our society. ❻<u>Dr. Stephen Hawking argued that</u> humans would be replaced by AI.

2. In the same conversation, if you find any evidence from an outside source, highlight it.

Step 3. This time, take a different stance from your partner and do a little research. Find more evidence and write a dialogue with your partner.

Step 4. Read the dialogue aloud with your partner.

Step 5. Then, try to come to a conclusion. Whether you come to the same conclusions or not, write the reason why.

Example

- We reached the same conclusion. Both of us agree with the statement mainly because···

- We did not reach the same conclusion. One agrees with the statement mainly because···, and the other disagrees with it mainly because···

Step 6. Next, form a new group with three other students and have a new discussion about your ideas. You are free to take either side and use any evidence you used in Step 3.

Research Presentation and Writing

Find your own topics for a research presentation or writing related to the unit's theme, or use one of the ones from below:

1. Machine learning
2. Deep learning algorithms
3. AI chatbot

Business: The Sharing Economy

Car Sharin

Introduction

🎧 1-10

A Listen to the following news story and fill in the blanks.

In June 2018, Mercari Inc. was listed on the Tokyo Stock Exchange. The company offers an online ¹( ) market platform that connects consumers who want to ²( ) goods and those who want to ³( ) them. The company was founded in ⁴( ), and at the end of ⁵( ), its app, Mercari, had had more than ⁶( )( ) downloads worldwide. One reason Mercari has ⁷( ) so quickly is that the company designed the app "with first-time sellers in mind." This means that the company tried to catch the attention of people who sell their goods for the ⁸( ) time. According to Mercari U.S., there are so many items in the average ⁹( ) that are no longer used. However, a lot of people think that selling these items is difficult and takes too much time. It can be said that the app helped change the ¹⁰( ) of such people by showing how easy selling an item is.

5

10

B The following are key phrases for the topic. Look them up in your dictionary and write the meanings.

1. between consumers   _____
2. act as a platform   _____
3. download an application (app)   _____
4. sign up to   _____
5. charge the provider handling fees   _____
6. carry out transactions   _____
7. eco-friendly and cost-effective   _____

C What do you see in these pictures? Talk about it with your partner.

1.
2.
3.

The sharing economy is expanding. Definitions of it can vary, but the term here refers to the buying and selling of goods and services between consumers by using applications (apps). The app acts as a platform that connects consumers. Using an app, anyone can buy and sell personal goods or services. The goods can be things like

5 bags or clothes, and the services could include offering a car ride or a room. In order to do this, you have to download an app and sign up to the system. It will ask you to register your name, address, and your credit card number. The transactions are easy to carry out by using a smartphone, and the prices are often reasonable. The companies that offer the app charge the provider handling fees. In this way, the sharing system is

10 convenient for all the participants.

A typical example of the sharing economy is Mercari. Using the Mercari app, people can buy and sell second-hand goods easily. Another example is Uber. Using the Uber app, a person who needs a ride and a driver who is nearby are matched instantly. Airbnb is another example. People can rent and use private rooms. For

15 instance, an owner of a house can rent his or her vacant rooms to tourists. In Japan, this service is called *minpaku*.

Although the sharing economy is eco-friendly and cost-effective, the quality may not be what you expect. Garments may have stains or holes, and rooms may be dirty. There are local regulations that limit such transactions, too. Uber drivers,

20 unlike licensed taxi drivers, are not professionals. Regulations in Japan do not allow nonprofessional drivers to transport paying customers. In the case of Airbnb in Japan, the owners have to register their rooms with their local governments and they are not supposed to rent these rooms for more than 180 days per year.

A Read the passage and answer the questions.

1. What is the definition of the sharing economy here?

_____

2. In what ways is the system convenient for all participants?

_____

3. In what ways is the buying and selling system inconvenient?

_____

B Complete an outline of the reading passage.

I. The sharing economy
  A. Definition
    1. It can be defined as "buying and selling of _____ and _____ between consumers using smartphone applications (apps)."
    2. The apps connect consumers by acting as a _____.
  B. How it works
    1. Download an _____.
    2. Sign up to the system.
    3. Register your name, address, and _____ number.
    4. Carry out transactions using a _____.
    5. Prices are _____.
    6. App companies charge the provider _____.

II. Typical examples
  A. Mercari
    1. People can buy and sell _____ goods.
  B. Uber
    1. A person who needs a _____ and a driver who can offer the ride are matched.
  C. Airbnb
    1. People can rent and use _____ rooms.
    2. This system is called _____ in Japan.

III. Inconveniences of the sharing economy
  A. The _____ of goods and services may be disappointing.
    1. You may find _____ or _____ in the product.
    2. You may find the offered room _____.
  B. Local _____ may limit the service.
    1. Taxi drivers should be _____.
    2. Minpaku rooms should be _____.
       The maximum length of stay should be _____ days per year.

A Study the figure and fill in the blanks.

 1-14

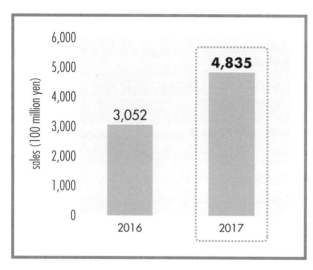

Figure 1: Estimated market scale of flea market applications

Source: Ministry of Economy, Trade and Industry (METI) "Internet Buying Boom: METI Releases Results of FY2017 E-Commerce Market Survey" https://www.meti.go.jp/english/press/2018/0425_002.html

Types	Business examples	Estimated market scale
Space	*Minpaku*, parking	140~180 (billion yen)
Goods	Flea market apps	300
Skill and Time	Housekeeping service	15~25
Money	Crowd funding	15~20

Table 1: Types of sharing economy and its market scale 2016

Source: 内閣府 経済社会総合研究所「シェアリングエコノミー等新分野の経済活動の計測に関する調査研究」より作成 http://www.esri.go.jp/jp/prj/hou/hou078/hou78.pdf

Figure 1 shows the estimated market scale of flea market apps in Japan. The source is a report by the Ministry of Economy, Trade and Industry (METI). The vertical axis shows the amount of sales in units of [1]( )( ) yen, which is *oku* in Japanese, and the horizontal axis shows the years, which are
5 [2]( ) and [3]( ). According to METI's report, flea market apps were first developed in Japan in 2012. The bar graph shows that in only four years, sales using these apps reached [4]( ) billion yen in 2016, while it increased to [5]( ) billion yen in 2017. This means that sales rose by more than [6]( ) percent between 2016 and 2017.

10 Table 1 shows the market scale in 2016 according to types of the sharing economy reported by the Cabinet Office. The biggest market is that of [7]( ), followed by space, which was estimated to be [8]( ) billion and 140 to 180 billion yen, respectively.

NOTES

market scale 市場規模　METI 経済産業省　vertical axis 縦軸　horizontal axis 横軸
Cabinet Office 内閣府

B Study the figure and fill in the blanks.

 1-15

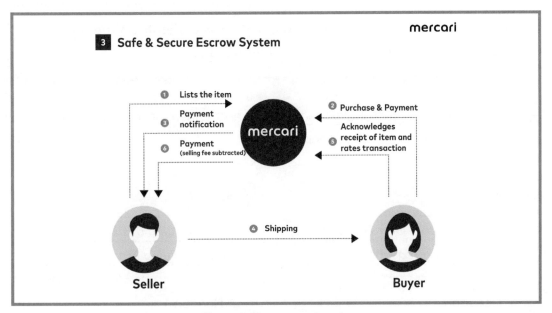

Figure 2: How mercari works

Source: mercari "FY2019.6 1Q Presentation Material Jul.2018-Sep. 2018" 2018年9月時点
https://pdf.irpocket.com/C4385/xouG/iyVp/bvOO.pdf

A: Recently, I sold some porcelain plates using Mercari.

B: I heard that it's easy to sell goods once you download the app.

A: That's true. Take a look at this flow chart. After signing up, first, I [1](   )
my plates on the app. I took photos of them and set the price. It was easy.

B: So, the buyer was able to see your plates clearly with the price.   5

A: Exactly. The buyer liked the plates and [2](   ) them. The payment
was made to Mercari. I received the [3](   ), so I [4](   ) my
plates. I took great care when I packed them because they were fragile.

B: I'm sure you did. So, when did you get paid?

A: Well, it was after the buyer [5](   ) the receipt of my plates. I got 10
paid online from Mercari later. The buyer [6](   ) the transaction, too. I was
happy that I got a high rating.

B: Did you have to pay anything to sell your plates?

A: Yeah, I paid a selling [7](   ) to Mercari. It was ten percent of the sale price.
The amount was [8](   ) from the transfer.   15

NOTES

porcelain 陶器　fragile 壊れやすい　subtract 差し引く

Discussion

A Agree or disagree?

> **Various flea market apps ("*furima-apuri*") are available online. The use of such apps will create a huge recycling market.**

Step 1. Do you agree or disagree with the above idea? Write two or three reasons supporting each side.

Agree

> *I agree with this idea because of the following reasons.*

✓ Reason 1

....
....
....

✓ Reason 2

....
....
....
....

✓ Reason 3

....
....
....
....

Disagree

> *I disagree with this idea because of the following reasons.*

✓ Reason 1

....
....
....

✓ Reason 2

....
....
....
....

✓ Reason 3

....
....
....
....

Step 2.   Learn the discussion strategies.

 1-16、17

1. In pairs, read out the following conversation. Write the numbers of the underlined expressions in the appropriate discussion strategies below.

Agreeing ____   Not sure ____

Asking for more explanations ____   Referring to a source ____

Giving your opinion ____

• *Example 1:*

A: Do you know about *furima-apuri*?

B: Yes, I do.

A: Do you think their popularity will create a huge recycling market?

B: **❶**I would say that it is possible. **❷**The Ministry of Economy, Trade and Industry reported that sales using flea market apps were as much as 483.5 billion yen in 2017. That's an increase of more than 50 percent from 2016. I think these kinds of apps are really popular!

A: **❸**I totally agree with you. It's so easy to sell things you don't use anymore. More people will use the apps in the future, so the market will grow.

• *Example 2:*

A: Do you think the use of flea market apps will lead to a large expansion of the recycling market?

B: **❹**Actually, I don't know. I hear that there are problems.

A: **❺**Could you give me an example?

B: **❻**I heard on the news that the clothes sold sometimes had holes or stains.

2. In the same conversation, if you find any evidence from an outside source, highlight it.

Step 3. This time, take a different stance from your partner and do a little research. Find more evidence and write a dialogue with your partner.

Step 4. Read the dialogue aloud with your partner.

Step 5. Then, try to come to a conclusion. Whether you come to the same conclusions or not, write the reason why.

Example

- **We reached the same conclusion. Both of us agree with the statement mainly because…**

- **We did not reach the same conclusion. One agrees with the statement mainly because…, and the other disagrees with it mainly because…**

Step 6. Next, form a new group with three other students and have a new discussion about your ideas. You are free to take either side and use any evidence you used in Step 3.

Research Presentation and Writing

Find your own topics for a research presentation or writing related to the unit's theme, or use one of the ones from below:

1. A comparison of different flea market apps
2. The use of Uber around the world
3. The pros and cons of Airbnb

UNIT 3

Food Waste:
Food Waste and Consumers

A **Listen to the following news story and fill in the blanks.**

A Japanese ¹(   ) chain, Genki Sushi, is getting rid of its conveyor belts. Instead, it will focus on direct, custom ²(   ). About 80 percent of the restaurants in the Genki chain now have tableside ³(   ) that customers can use to order with just a few taps of their finger. The sushi is prepared in the kitchen and placed on a ⁴(   ), and the plate is then in turn placed on a lane ₅ that quickly slides the order to the ⁵(   ). The company is planning to introduce this new system to all of its branches within ⁶(   ) years. This will result in fresher food for customers, less food ⁷(   ), and lower electricity consumption.

B **The following are key phrases for the topic. Look them up in your dictionary and write the meanings.**

1. throw the leftovers away   _____
2. concerned about the freshness and security   _____
3. the expiration date has passed   _____
4. offered on a conveyor belt   _____
5. go around the sushi lane   _____
6. ensure all the sushi is fresh and safe   _____
7. reduce the amount of sushi waste   _____

C **What do you see in these pictures? Talk about it with your partner.**

1.
2.
3.

29

5　　We produce a lot of food waste at home every day. At each meal, if some food is left uneaten, you may throw the leftovers away. This happens when you cook more than you can eat. If you don't check what food you have in your refrigerator before you go shopping, you may buy more than you need. Also, if you buy larger amounts of food in sets at bargain prices, you may buy too much. As a result, you will have more food than you need at home. Some of the food will expire and you will end up throwing it away.

10　　A lot of food waste is also produced at convenience stores, such as Seven-Eleven and FamilyMart every day. Customers are concerned about the freshness and safety of the food, so they like to buy newer and fresher products. Older products are more likely to be left unsold at the end of the day and when the expiration date has passed, they are thrown away. Moreover, to satisfy customers' wants and needs, stores always have a certain amount of food in stock. They also place various kinds of food products on the shelves. More food is always on display than the amount customers

15　buy, so unsold expired food is thrown away.

20　　At *kaiten-sushi* restaurants, sushi is offered on a conveyor belt and it goes around the sushi lane until it is taken by customers. If it is on the lane for too long, it is removed and thrown away to ensure all the sushi is fresh and safe. However, the restaurants have to throw a great amount of old sushi away. To reduce the amount of waste, restaurants keep track of customers' buying behavior and use past sales data. Kurasushi says it has reduced sushi waste to only 3 percent. Because of such efforts, restaurants have been successful in reducing waste.

A　Read the passage and answer the questions.

1.　If you have more food than you need at home, what happens next?

_____

2. Why do stores always have a certain amount of food in stock?

_____

3. Why is sushi removed and thrown away if it is on the lane for too long?

_____

B Complete an outline of the reading passage.

I. Food waste at home

    A. If some food is left uneaten, the _____ are thrown away.

    B. If you don't know what food you have in your _____, you may buy more than you need.

    C. You may buy larger amounts of food in _____ at _____.

II. Food waste at convenience stores

    A. Customers are concerned about the _____ and _____ of their food.

    B. Old products are thrown away when the _____ has passed.

    C. More food than the amount customers buy is always on _____

III. Food waste at *kaiten-sushi* restaurants

    A. Food waste

        1. If sushi is on the lane for too long, it is _____ and _____.

        2. It is to ensure all the sushi is _____ and _____.

    B. Restaurants' efforts

        1. Restaurants keep track of customers' _____.

        2. Restaurants use past _____.

Data

A Study the figure and fill in the blanks.

 1-22

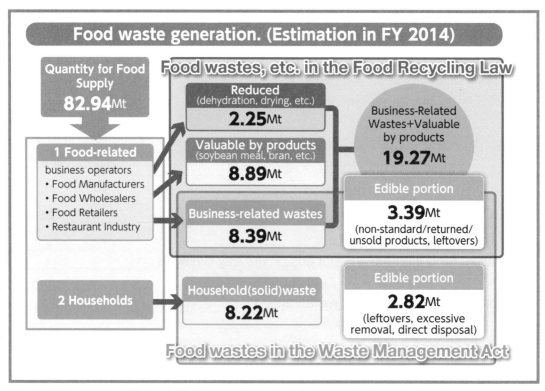

Figure 1: Food waste generation (Estimation in FY2014)

Source: MAFF "Reducing Food Loss and Waste & Promoting Recycling"
http://www.maff.go.jp/e/policies/env/attach/pdf/index-5.pdf

This figure shows [1](   ) (   ) estimation in the [2](   ) fiscal year. Food waste is divided into two groups. One is waste produced at [3](   ) (   ) (   ), such as food manufacturers, food wholesalers, food retailers, and the restaurant industry. The other is waste

5 produced by [4](   ). In 2014, the amount of the [5](   ) portion of food waste produced by food-related business operators was [6](   ) million tons. The products were non-standard, [7](   ), unsold, or leftovers. The edible portion of the food waste at home was [8](   ) million tons. It included [9](   ), excessive removal and direct disposal. About

10 [10](   ) percent of the edible portion of food waste was produced at home.

NOTES

manufactures 製造業者　wholesalers 卸し売り業者　retailers 小売り業者

B Study the figure and fill in the blanks.

 1-23

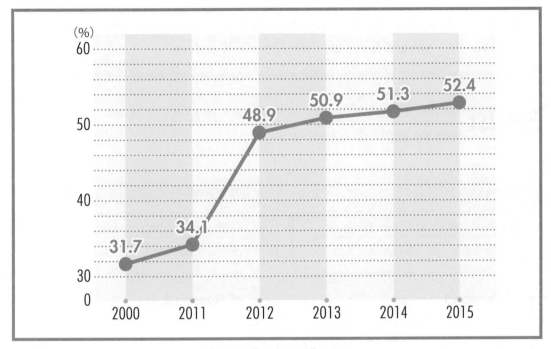

Figure 2: Food recycling rate

Source: 株式会社セブン・イレブン・ジャパン「環境への取り組み　食品リサイクル促進」より作成
https://www.sej.co.jp/social/eco/sales/food.html

A: Seven-Eleven says the company is making efforts to reduce the amount of food waste.

B: How will it do that?

A: By using various sales data. This data estimates the amount of food products to sell. 5

B: I see. But still, stores stock more products than customers buy, and some products will be left unsold.

A: Right. When the "sell-by" date has passed, the company has been collecting and [1]( ) those products since 1994. What do you think they are recycled into? 10

B: I read that they're recycled into [2]( ) to make plants grow and [3]( ) for animals. Do you know what percentage of the food is recycled?

A: More than [4]( ) of the food is now recycled and the food recycling rate is [5]( ) steadily. In 2015, it reached [6]( ) percent.

NOTES

estimate 概算する　sell-by date 販売期限

Discussion

A Agree or disagree?

Kaiten-sushi restaurants should stop offering sushi on a conveyor belt. Instead, they should focus on direct, custom orders.

Step 1. <u>Do you agree or disagree with the above idea?</u> Write two or three reasons supporting each side.

Agree	Disagree
I agree with this idea because of the following reasons.	*I disagree with this idea because of the following reasons.*

✓ Reason 1

....
....
....
....

✓ Reason 2

....
....
....
....

✓ Reason 3

....
....
....
....

✓ Reason 1

....
....
....
....

✓ Reason 2

....
....
....
....

✓ Reason 3

....
....
....
....

Step 2. | Learn the discussion strategies.

 1-24、25

1. In pairs, read out the following conversation. Write the numbers of the underlined expressions in the appropriate discussion strategies below.

Referring to a source ____   Starting a discussion ____

Agreeing ____   Asking for an opinion ____

Giving your opinion ____   Disagreeing ____

- *Example 1:*

   A: ❶What do you think about stopping offering sushi on a conveyor belt?

   B: I agree with this idea. We don't usually take sushi from the lane at *kaiten-sushi*.

   A: ❷That's a good point. Most customers order sushi by using a tablet. According to Genki Sushi, by focusing on custom orders, the sushi chain can reduce waste and it saves the chain about 100 million yen.

- *Example 2:*

   A: ❸Today's topic is food waste.

   B: ❹My opinion is that it's a good idea to stop offering sushi on a conveyor belt because the restaurants can reduce the amount of waste.

   A: ❺That may be true, but I disagree with this idea. Some restaurants still offer sushi on a conveyor belt. ❻I read that information technology has made it possible to track sales in real time and the restaurants have been successful in reducing the amount of waste.

2. In the same conversation, if you find any evidence from an outside source, highlight it.

Step 3. This time, take a different stance from your partner and do a little research. Find more evidence and write a dialogue with your partner.

Step 4. Read the dialogue aloud with your partner.

Step 5. Then, try to come to a conclusion. Whether you come to the same conclusions or not, write the reason why.

> **Example**
>
> • **We reached the same conclusion. Both of us agree with the statement mainly because···**
>
> • **We did not reach the same conclusion. One agrees with the statement mainly because···, and the other disagrees with it mainly because···**

Step 6. Next, form a new group with three other students and have a new discussion about your ideas. You are free to take either side and use any evidence you used in Step 3.

Research Presentation and Writing

Find your own topics for a research presentation or writing related to the unit's theme, or use one of the ones from below:

1. Food banks
2. Food sharing applications
3. Food tech

UNIT 4

Environmental Problems: Plastic Waste

Introduction

A Listen to the following news story and fill in the blanks.

In 2019, Prime Minister Shinzo Abe began to seek an international agreement to ¹(   ) plastic waste at the World ²(   ) Forum and the ³(   ) summit. Following the ⁴(   ) of plastic straws by Starbucks and Skylark Holdings, the government created a new movement in Japan. Since the 1970s, it is estimated that a huge amount of plastic waste has ⁵(   ) in the ocean between Hawaii and California. This island of plastic is called the Great Pacific Garbage Patch. Additionally, plastic bags have been found in the stomachs of dead ⁶(   ), and plastic straws in sea ⁷(   ). According to research in 2018, there were ⁸(   ) tons of plastic waste in the Great Pacific Garbage Patch, which was four to 16 times more than previously estimated.

5

10

B The following are key phrases for the topic. Look them up in your dictionary and write the meanings.

1. decrease (reduce) plastic waste   _____

2. is estimated   _____

3. conduct a survey   _____

4. affect the eco-system   _____

5. produce carbon dioxide emissions   _____

C What do you see in these pictures? Talk about it with your partner.

1.

2.

3.

In 2015, scientists of the Ocean Cleanup Foundation conducted a survey, using 30 boats with nets crossing the ocean at the same time. As a result, they collected 1.2 million plastic samples. After that, a military plane equipped with advanced technology, was used to spot large plastic objects in the ocean and measure the
5   garbage's density. They found that the Great Pacific Garbage Patch was 1.6 million km^2, about 4.2 times the size of Japan. Ninety-two percent of the area was made up of large objects, and it is estimated that they will break down into microplastics over the next few decades. It is a matter of great concern for everyone.

      Microplastics contain tiny pieces of industrial raw material called "resin
10 pellets" as well as broken pieces of large objects such as plastic containers. These microplastics absorb harmful chemicals while floating in the sea. If fish and other marine life eat them, this could lead to a disruption of their ecosystems, and the subsequent effects on the food chain could eventually impact human health. In October 2018, a research team led by Vienna Medical University reported that
15 microplastics had been found in human bodies for the first time. Microplastics are less than 5 mm in diameter, and have already been found in tap water, salt, and fish in various countries.

      Plastic waste does not decompose quickly. Plastic bags take 20 years, styrene foam 50 years, plastic bottles 450 years, diapers 450 years, and fishing lines 600 years. To
20 help remedy this situation, the Bio-Plastic Association in Japan has developed two kinds of environmentally friendly plastic called "bio-plastics." One is biodegradable which means it can be dissolved by microorganisms in the soil. Another is a biomass plastic, made from plant materials such as corn oil, that produces zero carbon dioxide emissions when they are incinerated. However, producing bio-plastics is still
25 expensive so they are not yet used widely around the world.

A Read the passage and answer the questions

1. What kind of survey did the Ocean Cleanup Foundation do?

_____

2. Why are microplastics a great concern for everyone?

_____

3. What are bio-plastics?

_____

B Complete an outline of the reading passage.

I. The survey of the Ocean Cleanup Foundation

  A. Using _____ with nets crossing the ocean at the same time

   1. _____ plastic samples

  B. Using a military _____ equipped with advanced technology to spot large plastic objects and measure the garbage's _____

   1. They found the Great Pacific Garbage Patch was _____ km^2.

   2. They found _____ of it is made up of large objects.

   3. It is estimated that these large objects will break down into _____ for the next few decades.

II. Microplastics -- a great concern for everyone

  A. What are microplastics?

   1. Very tiny pieces of resin pellets

   2. _____ of large objects, such as plastic containers

  B. They absorb _____ chemicals while floating in the sea.

  C. Bad effects

   1. They might affect _____ and human health.

   2. They were found in the human bodies in 2018.

   3. They have been found in tap water, _____, and _____ in various countries.

III. Plastic waste does not decompose easily.

  A. Years required

   1. Plastic bags take 20 years, styrene foam 50 years, plastic bottles 450 years, diapers 450 years, and fishing lines _____ years.

  B. The Bio-Plastic Association in Japan has developed:

   1. _____

    a. A _____ plastic can be dissolved by microorganisms in the soil.

    b. A biomass plastic is made from _____ materials such as corn oil, which produces zero _____ emissions.

    c. They are still _____ and not used widely around the world yet.

Data

A Study the figures and fill in the blanks.

 1-30

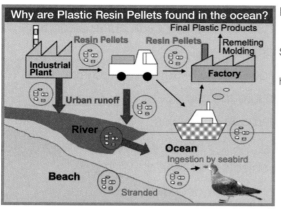

Figure 1: Why are Plastic Resin Pellets found in the ocean?

Source: International Pellet Watch "Why Plastic Resin Pellets are found in the Ocean?"
http://www.pelletwatch.org/en/what.html

Figure 2: Worst Plastic Offenders

Source: CLIMATEDESK "Worst Plastic Offenders." Data from Jambeck et al. 2015
https://grist.org/living/theres-a-scary-amount-of-plastic-in-the-ocean-heres-who-put-it-there/

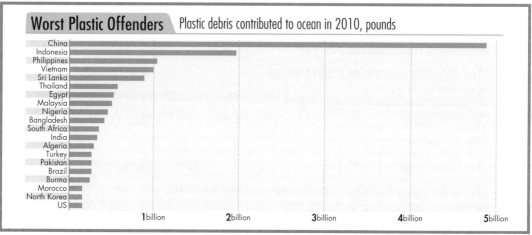

Figure 1 shows why plastic resin pellets are found in the ocean. Since they are very small, they can be released into the environment from ¹( ) plants when they are produced, and from cars used for transportation to ²( ), where they are molded into the final plastic products. After, they flow into
5 ³( ) as a result of rainfall and eventually reach the ⁴( ). Seabirds might eat them.

Figure 2 shows the top ⁵( ) countries who dumped plastic waste into the ocean in 2010. ⁶( ) was at the top, dumping nearly ⁷( ) billion pounds of plastic waste, which weighs about 2.26 billion kg. After China, there
10 were many Asian and ⁸( ) countries listed. It is believed that they were middle-income countries with growing populations in coastal areas, and they did not have the resources to deal with the plastic waste. Among developed countries, ⁹( ) was included because each person disposed of a large amount of waste.

NOTES

offenders 違反者　resin pellets 樹脂ペレット　transportation 運送　mold 成形をする
dump 投げ捨てる　dispose of 投げ捨てる

B Study the figure and fill in the blanks.

 1-31

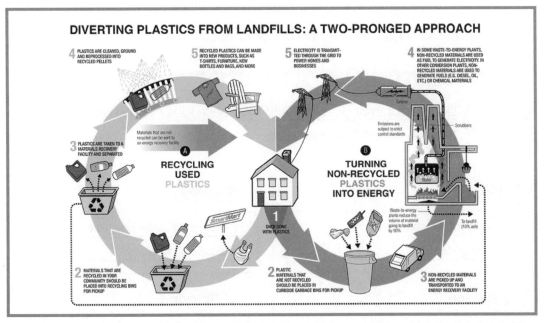

Figure 3: "Plastics Make it Possible" Published in September, 2011 and updated in October, 2018

Source: American Chemistry Council "How to Divert Plastics from Landfills"
https://www.plasticsmakeitpossible.com/whats-new-cool/technology-science/plastics-to-energy/how-to-divert-plastics-from-landfills/ (Published on September 21, 2011Article updated on October 24, 2018)

A: Figure 3 shows [1]( ) approaches for recycling of plastic waste. Did you know that there are the four "R's" involved in the reduction of plastic waste?

B: Reduce, reuse, recycle and …

A: Recovery.

B: Recovery? What does that mean?   5

A: Energy recovery. The right-hand circle shows this. Non-recycled plastic is sent to a facility to be converted into electricity, which powers [2]( ) and [3]( ). In the US, 13 percent of waste is processed to produce electricity with cleaner emissions.

B: That's ideal, if the process does not emit carbon dioxide.   10

A: Yes. And the left-hand circle shows the ordinary recycling process. In the end, plastic waste can be changed into T-shirts, [4]( ), new bottles and [5]( ).

B: Creating clothing from plastic [6]( ) is amazing! Technology helps us a lot.   15

⌐ NOTES ⌐

divert 転用する　landfills 埋立地　pronged 分けた　recovery 再生（利用）　convert into 変化させる
process 加工・処理する

Discussion

A Agree or disagree?

We should live without using plastic products.

Step 1. Do you agree or disagree with the above idea? Write two or three reasons supporting each side.

Agree

I agree with this idea for the following reasons.

✓ Reason 1

....
....
....
....

✓ Reason 2

....
....
....
....

✓ Reason 3

....
....
....
....

Disagree

I disagree with this idea for the following reasons.

✓ Reason 1

....
....
....
....

✓ Reason 2

....
....
....
....

✓ Reason 3

....
....
....
....

Step 2. | Learn the discussion strategies.   CD 1-32、33

1. In pairs, read out the following conversation. Write the numbers of the underlined expressions in the appropriate discussion strategies below.

Agreeing ____   Starting a discussion ____

Showing examples ____   Giving a solution ____

Disagreeing ____   Referring to a source ____

• *Example 1:*

A: What do you think about using plastic products?

B: I disagree with this idea because sometimes it is impossible to avoid using plastic.

A: ❶You can say that again. We can't go back to a world without plastic products.

B: No, we can't. Rather, ❷we should try to help clean up plastic waste and develop technology to exploit it.

• *Example 2:*

A: ❸Today's topic is whether we should live without using plastic products.

B: I agree with this idea because we know that plastic waste pollutes our society. ❹For instance, ❺Ocean Cleanup, the Holland-based NGO, reported that there were 80,000 tons of plastic waste in the Pacific Ocean in 2018.

A: ❻That may be true, but I disagree with this idea because living without plastic products is not realistic and bad for the economy.

2. In the same conversation, if you find any evidence from an outside source, highlight it.

Step 3. This time, take a different stance from your partner and do a little research. Find more evidence and write a dialogue with your partner.

Step 4. Read the dialogue aloud with your partner.

Step 5. Then, try to come to a conclusion. Whether you come to the same conclusions or not, write the reason why.

Example

- **We reached the same conclusion. Both of us agree with the statement mainly because···**

- **We did not reach the same conclusion. One agrees with the statement mainly because···, and the other disagrees with it mainly because···**

Step 6. Next, form a new group with three other students and have a new discussion about your ideas. You are free to take either side and use any evidence you used in Step 3.

Research Presentation and Writing

Find your own topics for a research presentation or writing related to the unit's theme, or use one of the ones from below:

1. Recent situations regarding plastic waste
2. New technology for getting rid of plastic waste
3. Other environmental problems:
   a. discarded clothing
   b. air pollution
   c. e-trash (electronic waste)

UNIT 5

The Japanese Mentality: Do They Have Good Manners?

Introduction

 1-34

A **Listen to the following news story and fill in the blanks.**

In 2019, ¹(   ) education at junior high schools was upgraded to an official ²(   ) from an extracurricular subject. The new ethics ³(   ) were released by eight publishers and they all deal with current topics in Japan. For example, they cover moral issues related to ⁴(   ) technology, such as ⁵(   ) through the use of smartphones and social media. Other topics are the Great East Japan Earthquake in 2011, which devastated coastal areas of northern Japan, and a series of powerful ⁶(   ) that mainly hit Kumamoto Prefecture in 2016. Furthermore, the newest topics are voter education, and the 2020 Tokyo ⁷(   ) and Paralympics.

5

B **The following are key phrases for the topic. Look them up in your dictionary and write the meanings.**

1. imagine other people's feelings   _____
2. good manners   _____
3. kept calm   _____
4. waited in lines   _____
5. priority seats   _____
6. moral education   _____
7. charitable organizations   _____

C **What do you see in these pictures? Talk about it with your partner.**

1.

2.

3.

Omoiyari is said to be a key concept of the Japanese mentality. Its primary meaning is the ability to imagine other people's feelings. Japanese people's good manners have often been associated with it and reported in news articles. For example, Japanese soccer supporters cleaned up the stadium after the matches at the World
5　Cup, actions that were praised by the foreign media. Some experts say the supporters' behavior is related to education in Japan, where children clean their classrooms every day. Another example was seen during the frequent natural disasters. Even in such situations, many people still kept calm and patiently waited in lines for emergency supplies.

10　However, there are now numerous instances of Japanese people's bad manners. According to a survey by an organization to promote good manners in Tokyo, less than 30 percent of Tokyo residents think people in Tokyo have good manners. For example, Tokyo residents notice bad manners on the train. Some young people sit in priority seats and do not give up their seats to the elderly, and others put on makeup.
15　In an effort to get the passengers to act more politely, railway companies display posters, saying things such as, "Please line up and wait your turn" or "Please switch your phone to silent mode while riding the train."

Omoiyari is often seen in school mottoes and emphasized in moral education at school. Some of the values that students are taught include respecting the elderly,
20　helping those with disabilities, and keeping promises. Students also take turns being in charge of cleaning the classroom, serving lunch, taking care of plants and animals. In addition, volunteer clubs collect money for charitable organizations and members visit elderly people in nursing homes. In moral education class, students read stories and discuss the topics in them. The teacher facilitates the discussion and the students
25　draw their own conclusions.

A Read the passage and answer the questions.

1. What is the primary meaning of *omoiyari*?

_____

2. What are some examples of Japanese people's bad manners?

_____

3. What do students do in moral education class at school?

_____

B Complete an outline of the reading passage.

I. *Omoiyari*

    A. A key concept of the Japanese mentality

        1. It is the _____ to imagine other people's feelings.

        2. Japanese people's _____ have been associated with it.

    B. Examples of good manners

        1. Japanese soccer supporters _____ up the stadium.

        2. People kept _____ and waited in _____ during disasters.

II. Bad manners

    A. Survey

        1. Less than _____ percent of Tokyo residents think they have good manners.

    B. Examples of bad manners

        1. People don't give up their seats to the _____ on the train.

        2. People put on _____ on the train.

    C. Campaigns

        1. Railway companies display _____.

III. *Omoiyari* in moral education at school

    A. Values

        1. Students learn about respecting the _____.

        2. Students learn about helping people with _____.

        3. Students learn about keeping _____.

    B. Activities

        1. Students _____ the classroom.

        2. Students _____ lunch.

        3. Students take care of _____ and _____.

        4. The volunteer club collects money for _____.

        5. The volunteer club visits elderly people in _____.

    C. Moral education class

        1. Students _____ stories and _____ the topics.

        2. The teacher _____ the discussion.

        3. Students draw their own _____.

Data

A Study the figure and fill in the blanks.

 1-38

Americans, Japanese See Each Other Through Different Lenses

Which characteristics do you associate with _____

	American views of Japanese	Japanese views of Americans (%)
Hardworking	94	25
Inventive	75	67
Honest	71	37
Intolerant	36	29
Aggressive	31	50
Selfish	19	47

Figure 1: Americans, Japanese See Each Other Through Different Lenses

Source: Pew Research Center "How Americans and Japanese see each other"
https://www.pewresearch.org/fact-tank/2015/04/09/how-americans-and-japanese-see-each-other/

Figure 1 shows how the American and Japanese people see each other. The former three characteristics show positive impressions and the latter three characteristics show [1]( ) ones. Ninety-four percent of Americans think the Japanese are [2]( ) and [3]( ) percent of Americans see
5 the Japanese as inventive. Seventy-one percent of them also see the Japanese as [4]( ). Based on this data, Americans have fewer [5]( ) stereotypes of the Japanese. In contrast, the [6]( ) tend to be more critical of [7]( ). Only 37 percent of Japanese associate honesty with Americans and only 25 percent say Americans are [8]( ). At the
10 same time, [9]( ) percent say Americans are aggressive and 47 percent see them as [10]( ).

B Study the figure and fill in the blanks.

 1-39

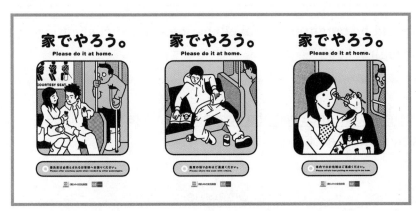

Figure 2:
Tokyo Metro: "Please do it at home."

Source:
東京メトロマナーポスター「家で やろう。」
https://www.tokyometro.jp/ news/2008/2008-16.html

A: Many foreign people see Japanese people as having good manners. Do you think this is true?

B: I think it's not always true. I sometimes see people's [1](   ) manners on the train. Look at Figure 2. Tokyo Metro created a series of posters to promote good [2](   ) on the train. The posters are based on facts and you 5 will sometimes find people doing these things. Here are three examples of bad manners.

A: In the first poster, a man and a woman are sitting in a [3](   ) seat.

B: Who is the seat for?

A: It is for people who are elderly, pregnant, or injured. 10

B: Right. You can see an [4](   ) man standing by that seat. He is using a crutch. What should the two people do?

A: They should [5](   ) up their seat to the man?

B: That's right. In the second poster, you can see a man. Can you see any bad behavior? 15

A: He is taking up [6](   ).

B: You're right. There's enough space for one more person to [7](   ). In addition, he left empty [8](   ) on the floor and he is stretching out his [9](   ). In the third poster, you see a girl. What's she doing?

A: She's putting on [10](   ). 20

B: Right. Doing something like that in public places is considered to be bad manners.

NOTES

promote 推奨する pregnant 妊娠した crutch 松葉づえ

Discussion

A Agree or disagree?

> **Good manners should be taught in moral education class at elementary school and junior high school.**

Step 1. Do you agree or disagree with the above idea? Write two or three reasons supporting each side.

Agree

I agree with this idea because of the following reasons.

✓ Reason 1

....
....
....
....

✓ Reason 2

....
....
....
....

✓ Reason 3

....
....
....
....

Disagree

I disagree with this idea because of the following reasons.

✓ Reason 1

....
....
....
....

✓ Reason 2

....
....
....
....

✓ Reason 3

....
....
....
....

Step 2. Learn the discussion strategies. 1-40、41

1. In pairs, read out the following conversation. Write the numbers of the underlined expressions in the appropriate discussion strategies below.

Referring to a source ____   Starting a discussion ____

Agreeing ____   Asking for an opinion ____

Giving your opinion ____   Disagreeing ____

• *Example 1:*

A: Today we're going to discuss whether good manners should be taught in moral education class or not. ❶What do you think about this idea?

B: ❷In my opinion, good manners should be taught in moral education class because one of the goals of moral education is to teach children the rules of society.

A: ❸I totally agree with you. ❹As the Course of Study shows, students learn to keep promises, follow rules, and have a sense of public duty.

• *Example 2:*

A: Today's topic is whether good manners should be taught at school. ❺What's your stance on this idea?

B: I think teachers should teach good manners in class. For example, students can learn how to behave in public places such as stadiums and on the train.

A: ❻That's a good point, but experts say schools should not teach stereotypical values to students. I also think more time should be used to teach other subjects.

2. In the same conversation, if you find any evidence from an outside source, highlight it.

Step 3. This time, take a different stance from your partner and do a little research. Find evidence and write a dialogue with your partner.

Step 4. Read the dialogue aloud with your partner.

Step 5. Then, try to come to a conclusion. Whether you come to the same conclusions or not, write the reason why.

Example

- **We reached the same conclusion. Both of us agree with the statement mainly because…**

- **We did not reach the same conclusion. One agrees with the statement mainly because…, and the other disagrees with it mainly because…**

Step 6. Next, form a new group with three other students and have a new discussion about your ideas. You are free to take either side and use any evidence you used in Step 3.

Research Presentation and Writing

Find your own topics for a research presentation or writing related to the unit's theme, or use one of the ones from below:

1. Group-oriented society
2. Individualism
3. Seniority system

UNIT 6

Space Exploration: Will Space Benefit Our Future?

Introduction

🎵 1-42

A Listen to the following news story and fill in the blanks.

The Japanese space probe, Hayabusa 2, was sent into [1]( ) to examine a small [2]( ), Ryugu. Ryugu is 300 million km from the Earth. Hayabusa 2 approached Ryugu in June 2018 and it [3]( ) successfully on February 22, 2019. An observation robot was released first, and then Hayabusa 2 touched down on Ryugu. The planet is thought to contain organic matter and [4]( ) 5 from 4.6 billion years ago, when the [5]( ) system was born, so Hayabusa 2 may discover some of the earliest evidence of [6]( ). Hayabusa 2 collected [7]( ) samples, which will be brought back to the Earth by December [8]( ).

B The following are key phrases for the topic. Look them up in your dictionary and write the meanings.

1. private companies   _____
2. sounding rocket   _____
3. business opportunities   _____
4. launch services   _____
5. small satellites   _____
6. space debris   _____
7. artificial shooting stars _____

C What do you see in these pictures? Talk about it with your partner.

1.

2.

3.

In recent years, private companies have entered the field of space exploration, and Japanese companies are also playing a leading role. For example, on May 4, 2019, a small sounding rocket, Momo-3, was launched from its test site in Hokkaido and successfully reached outer space. The rocket was developed by a Japanese company,
5   Interstellar Technologies. It was the first successful launch of a rocket developed by a private company in Japan. Because government budgets have been shrinking, more companies are entering the market and they are participating in space exploration with an eye to seeking business opportunities.

Some companies are focusing on developing small rockets because they have
10 several advantages when carrying satellites into space. Large rockets cost more than small ones, so they cannot be launched so often and they usually carry several satellites at the same time. In a way, large rockets are like a bus service. Passengers cannot decide the departure time and they may have to wait, so it is not flexible. In contrast, a small rocket is like a taxi. Passengers can get on and get off anywhere
15 whenever they like. Therefore, there are high hopes for small, flexible rockets. Interstellar Technologies says its goal is to provide low-cost, reliable launch services of small rockets.

By launching small rockets more often, more satellites can be sent into space. In Japan, businesses using small satellites have started up. For example, Umitron
20 provides aquaculture support services using satellite data. By analyzing fish behavior and designing feeding amounts and timing, the company is trying to stop wasting feed and reduce costs. Astroscale develops technologies to remove space debris and protect the space environment. By monitoring debris from the Earth, the company aims to remove it. Another company, ALE intends to provide an entertainment
25 service. The company plans to create artificial shooting stars by using the heat of the atmosphere. It will release metal balls from a satellite into the night sky.

A Read the passage and answer the questions.

1. What companies have entered the field of space exploration?

_____

2. What is the goal of Interstellar Technologies?

_____

3. Which businesses related to space have started in Japan?

_____

B **Complete an outline of the reading passage.**

I. Private companies' participation

   A. Japanese companies

      1. _____ reached outer space.

      2. It was developed by _____.

      3. It was the first successful _____.

   B. Space industry

      1. It accepts more _____.

      2. _____ have been shrinking.

      3. Companies are seeking _____.

II. Developing small rockets

   A. Large rockets

      1. They cost _____.

      2. They _____ be launched often.

      3. They carry _____ at the same time.

      4. They are _____.

   B. Small rockets

      1. They are _____.

      2. Low-cost, reliable _____ are being developed.

III. Businesses using small satellites

   A. Umitron

      1. It provides _____.

      2. It is trying to _____.

   B. Astroscale

      1. It monitors _____ from the Earth.

      2. It aims to _____ the debris.

   C. ALE

      1. It intends to provide an _____.

      2. It plans to create _____.

A Study the figure and fill in the blanks.

 1-46

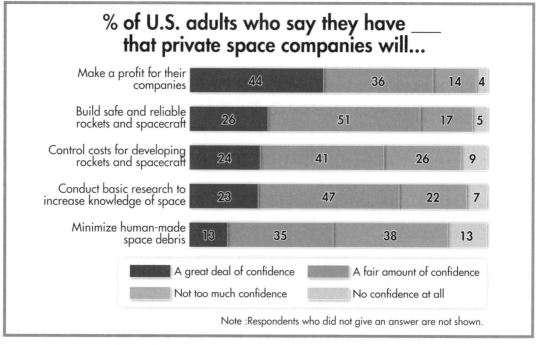

Figure 1: What Americans think of private space companies

Source: Pew Research center "Survey conducted March 27-Aprli 9, 2018"
https://www.pewresearch.org/fact-tank/2018/06/22/many-in-u-s-have-confidence-in-what-private-space-companies-will-accomplish/

Figure 1 shows what Americans think of [1]( ) space companies. A large majority of Americans are confident that the companies will make a [2]( ) from their ventures. [3]( ) percent of them have a great deal of confidence and an additional [4]( ) percent have a fair amount of
5 confidence. Also, Americans think these companies will contribute to the country's space exploration. [5]( ) percent of them have a great deal or a fair amount of confidence that the companies will build safe and reliable rockets and spacecraft. Sixty-five percent of them think the companies will control [6]( ) for developing rockets and spacecraft. Seventy percent of them think the
10 companies will conduct [7]( ) ( ) to increase knowledge and understanding of space. However, there is more skepticism about whether private companies will minimize human-made space debris. [8]( ) percent of them have at least a fair amount of confidence that the companies will minimize space debris, while [9]( ) percent of them have little or no confidence. Space
15 debris increasingly poses a hazard to orbiting satellites and space stations.

NOTES

ventures 事業　skepticism 懐疑　hazard 危険

B Study the figure and fill in the blanks.

 1-47

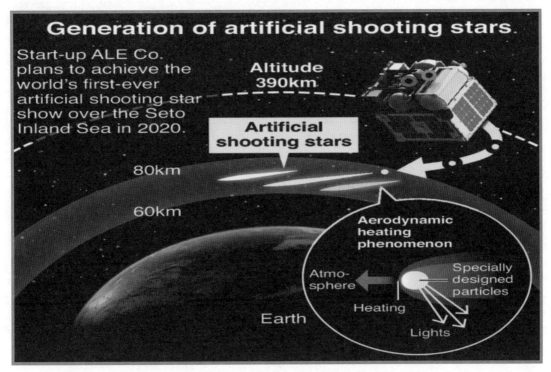

Figure 2: The new generation of artificial shooting stars

Source: Wishing upon an artificial shooting star / A succession of Japanese join the fray 2019.1.23 The Japan news

A: Japanese companies are planning a variety of projects in space. For example, a private satellite that will artificially [1]( ) shooting stars was launched for the first time in January 2019.

B: I heard that news. A space venture company based in Tokyo, ALE, plans to realize artificial shooting stars by using a small [2]( ). It is planned for 5 spring 2020 and the shooting stars will likely be visible over the Seto Inland Sea.

A: Do you know how it will be carried out?

B: Specially designed [3]( ) will be released from an altitude of [4]( ) kilometers from the [5]( ). The particles are around 1 centimeter in diameter and act as space dust. The particles will glow for 3 to 10 10 seconds at altitudes of 60 to [6]( ) kilometers in the air. They will be as bright as Sirius, the brightest star in the night sky.

A: How long will we be able to see those shooting stars?

B: The entire show is planned to last for about one minute.

NOTES

the Seto Inland Sea 瀬戸内海   altitude 高度   diameter 直径   glow 輝く

Discussion

A Agree or disagree?

> **Japan should promote more private-sector space ventures.**

Step 1. <u>Do you agree or disagree with the above idea?</u> Write two or three reasons supporting each side.

Agree

> *I agree with this idea because of the following reasons.*

✓ **Reason 1**

....
....
....
....

✓ **Reason 2**

....
....
....
....

✓ **Reason 3**

....
....
....
....

Disagree

> *I disagree with this idea because of the following reasons.*

✓ **Reason 1**

....
....
....
....

✓ **Reason 2**

....
....
....
....

✓ **Reason 3**

....
....
....
....

Step 2. Learn the discussion strategies.

 1-48、49

1. In pairs, read out the following conversation. Write the numbers of the underlined expressions in the appropriate discussion strategies below.

Referring to a source ____   Asking for an opinion ____

Agreeing ____   Disagreeing ____

Giving your opinion ____

- *Example 1:*

  A: ❶Don't you think it is a good idea to promote more private-sector space ventures?

  B: I agree with this idea. If more small satellites can be launched at lower prices, we will be able to use more data in our daily life.

  A: ❷Exactly. ❸According to Umitron, in aquaculture, data from the satellites will help cut costs. We will always be able to give just the right amount of feed to fish and avoid giving them more than they need. It will enable us to save money on feeding fish.

- *Example 2:*

  A: What's your opinion about promoting more private-sector space ventures?

  B: ❹In my view, private companies will revitalize space exploration.

  A: ❺You have a point there, but I'm against it. Launching more satellites means leaving more debris in space. I read that the amount of space debris is increasing, so we should stop polluting space.

2. In the same conversation, if you find any evidence from an outside source, highlight it.

Step 3. This time, take a different stance from your partner and do a little research. Find more evidence and write a dialogue with your partner.

Step 4. Read the dialogue aloud with your partner.

Step 5. Then, try to come to a conclusion. Whether you come to the same conclusions or not, write the reason why.

Example

- **We reached the same conclusion. Both of us agree with the statement mainly because···**

- **We did not reach the same conclusion. One agrees with the statement mainly because···, and the other disagrees with it mainly because···**

Step 6. Next, form a new group with three other students and have a new discussion about your ideas. You are free to take either side and use any evidence you used in Step 3

Research Presentation and Writing

Find your own topics for a research presentation or writing related to the unit's theme, or use one of the ones from below:

1. Rocket development and launch services
2. Satellite remote sensing service
3. Developing space resources

UNIT 7
Immigration: Foreign Residents in Japan

Introduction

🎵 1-50

A **Listen to the following news story and fill in the blanks.**

The government started a ¹(   ) survey of whether all foreign children living in Japan are ²(   ) school or not. In 2018, ³(   ) foreign children between the ages of six and ⁴(   ) were estimated to be not attending school in Japan. The number was calculated by a working group consisting of NHK and some experts. However, the exact number was ⁵(   ), 5 for the government had never checked it before. In Japan, the law requiring ⁶(   ) education does not apply to children of foreign residents. Therefore, their attendance at school has not been checked as carefully as that of Japanese children. The United Nations Convention on the Rights of the Child states that all children have the ⁷(   ) to be educated no matter what their 10 ⁸(   ) is. Because the number of foreign ⁹(   ) has been increasing, the government finally started a survey starting in 2019.

B **The following are key phrases for the topic. Look them up in your dictionary and write the meanings.**

1. compulsory education   _____
2. the status of foreign residents   _____
3. technical interns   _____
4. ease labor shortages   _____
5. a maximum five-year residency   _____
6. temporary workers   _____

C **What do you see in these pictures? Talk about it with your partner.**

1.
2.
3.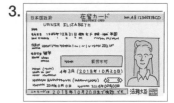

The number of foreign workers in Japan is increasing. According to the Ministry of Health, Labor and Welfare (MHLW), the number was nearly 1.3 million in 2018. The government's policy is to accept more foreign workers in order to ease labor shortages. In fact, a new visa status was created in April 2019. The status allows a

5 maximum five-year residency to foreigners who have specific skills in 14 industries including nursing and food service. The new status will provide the labor market with another 345 thousand foreign workers over a five-year period.

MHLW also reported that in 2018, 20 percent of foreign workers were technical interns. They came to Japan to learn specific skills under a national training program,

10 which was introduced in 1993. The program aims to contribute to developing countries by transferring job skills. The skills include manufacturing foods and clothes, and constructing buildings. The interns come from countries such as Vietnam, China, the Philippines, and Indonesia and are allowed to stay in Japan for up to five years. Some employers in the agricultural and fishery sectors say that their

15 businesses might fail without access to such workers.

Recently, accepting more foreign workers over a longer time span is under debate. If technical interns get the new status after acquiring a specific skill, they can be granted residency of up to 10 years. However, Professor Kiyoto Tanno of Tokyo Metropolitan University says that this is rather short. He warns that as long as

20 they are considered temporary workers, the skills they can learn are limited. Thus, many foreign workers will continue to fill shortages of low-wage workers. Actually, the poor working conditions for interns, such as low wages, long working hours, and poor safety measures have already become a serious problem. Tanno suggests that Japan should allow foreign workers to stay longer so that they can learn more

25 advanced skills. Otherwise, in the future, they may no longer choose Japan as a work destination.

A Read the passage and answer the questions.

1. Why is the government trying to accept more foreign residents?

_____

2. What is the aim of the technical intern program?

_____

3. What does Professor Tanno warn about? Why is it a problem?

_____

B Complete an outline of the reading passage.

I. Current situation of foreign workers in Japan

    A. The number of foreign workers

        1. It is increasing every year.

        2. It was nearly _____ in 2018.

    B. The government wants more workers.

        1. A new visa _____ was created in 2019.

        2. The maximum stay is five years.

        3. They are foreigners who have _____.

        4. The number of foreign workers will increase by 345 thousand.

II. Technical intern program

    A. The interns accounted for _____ of the foreign workers in 2018.

    B. It is a _____ training program.

        1. It aims to transfer _____ to developing countries.

        2. Interns come from _____, China, the Philippines, and

          _____.

        3. Their stay is maximum _____ years.

        4. Businesses in agricultural and fishery sectors might fail without such workers.

III. Debate for a longer time span for foreign workers

    A. Professor Tanno's warnings

        1. Foreign workers are _____ workers.

        2. The skills they can learn are limited.

        3. They fill shortages of _____.

        4. They work in _____ conditions.

    B. Professor Tanno's suggestion

        1. Let foreign workers stay longer.

        2. Let them learn more _____.

        3. Otherwise, they may no longer choose Japan as a work destination.

A Study the tables and fill in the blanks.

 1-54

Ranking	Origin	Number in 2018(June)	Number in 2017(June)	Percentage in 2018	Increase from 2017	Increase ratio from 2017
1	China	741,656	711,486	28.1	30,170	4.2
2	South Korea	452,701	452,953	17.2	▲252	▲0.1
3	Vietnam	291,494	232,562	11.1	58,932	25.3
4	Philippines	266,803	251,934	10.1	14,869	5.9
5	Brazil	196,781	185,967	7.5	10,814	5.8
6	Nepal	85,321	74,300	3.2	11,021	14.8
7	Taiwan	58,456	54,358	2.2	4,098	7.5
8	US	56,834	54,918	2.2	1,916	3.5
9	Indonesia	51,881	46,350	2.0	5,531	11.9

Table 1: The top 9 "countries of origin" for foreign residents in Japan

Ranking	Prefecture	Number in 2018(June)	Number in 2017(June)	Percentage in 2018	Increase from 2017	Increase ratio from 2017
1	Tokyo	555,053	512,088	21.0	33,965	6.5
2	Aichi	251,823	234,330	9.5	17,493	7.5
3	Osaka	233,713	223,025	8.9	10,688	4.8
4	Kanagawa	211,913	198,557	8.0	13,356	6.7
5	Saitama	173,887	160,026	6.6	13,861	8.7
6	Chiba	152,186	139,823	5.8	12,363	8.8
7	Hyogo	107,708	103,505	4.1	4,203	4.1
8	Shizuoka	88,720	83,093	3.4	5,627	6.8

Table 2: The top 8 prefectures where foreign residents lived in Japan

Source: 法務省「在留外国人統計（旧登録外国人統計）2018 年 6 月調査」より作成　https://www.e-stat.go.jp

Foreign residents are mid- to long-term residents from overseas including permanent residents. In 2018, there were more than 2.6 million foreign residents in Japan. Table 1 shows the number of them according to their country of origin. In 2018, the largest population was from [1](   ), which accounted for

5 [2](   ) percent of the total foreign residents. The second largest was from [3](   ) although the population showed a slight decrease from 2017. The country that showed the greatest increase from 2017 was [4](   ), which increased by [5](   ) percent. Residents from [6](   ) and [7](   ) also increased by 14.8 percent and 11.9 percent respectively.

10 Table 2 shows the most common prefectures foreign residents lived in. During 2017 and 2018, the top prefecture was [8](   ), followed by [9](   ), [10](   ), and Kanagawa. This shows that foreigners lived in the four most populous prefectures in Japan.

NOTES

permanent resident 永住者　country of origin 出身国　populous 人口が多い

B Study the figure and fill in the blanks.

 1-55

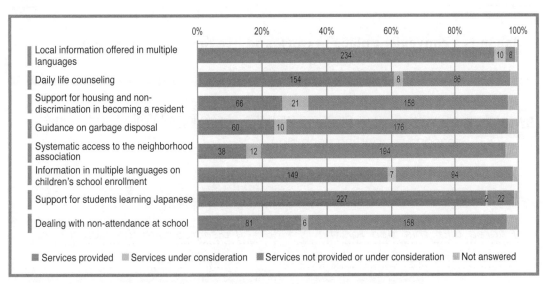

Figure 1: Services municipal offices offer to foreign residents

Source: 総務省「AI インクルージョン推進会議」第 1 回会議 資料 3、日本経済新聞の記事より富士通総研が作成したものより抜粋
http://www.soumu.go.jp/main_sosiki/kenkyu/ai_inclusion/02iicp01_04000177.html

A: Do you think foreign residents in Japan get enough support from their local municipal offices?

B: I've never thought about that. Living in Japan must be very different from living in their home countries. Foreign residents definitely need support, I guess.

A: They sure do. Take a look at Figure 1. It shows some of the ^1(   ) 5 municipal offices offer to foreign residents. More than 85 percent of the offices already offer information in ^2(   ) languages.

B: That's great. I wonder if foreign residents are able to get along with their neighbors easily.

A: Well, only 20 percent of the municipal offices are willing to help put them in 10 touch with the ^3(   ) (   ). I think neighbors can do a lot to support new residents, though.

B: How about information related to education? I've heard that quite a few foreign children living in Japan don't receive primary education.

A: Well, let's see. Nearly ^4(   ) percent of the municipal offices offer information 15 to foreign residents when their children enter school. Nearly 90 percent of them also help children learn ^5(   ). But... only about ^6(   ) percent of the municipal offices deal with children who actually don't go to school.

NOTES

municipal office 地方自治体   neighborhood association 自治会   school enrollment 入学手続き
multiple languages 多言語   non-discrimination 差別をしないこと   garbage disposal ごみ捨て
non-attendance 欠席

A Agree or disagree?

Japan is a convenient place to work and live for foreign residents.

Step 1. Do you agree or disagree with the above idea? Write two or three reasons supporting each side.

Agree

I agree with this idea for the following reasons:

✓ Reason 1

....
....
....
....

✓ Reason 2

....
....
....
....

✓ Reason 3

....
....
....
....

Disagree

I disagree with this idea for the following reasons:

✓ Reason 1

....
....
....
....

✓ Reason 2

....
....
....
....

✓ Reason 3

....
....
....
....

Step 2. Learn the discussion strategies.   🎧 1-56、57

1. In pairs, read out the following conversation. Write the numbers of the underlined expressions in the appropriate discussion strategies below.

Agreeing ____   **Showing examples** ____

Giving your opinion ____   **Adding ideas** ____

Disagreeing ____

• *Example 1:*

   A: Today's topic is about foreign residents in Japan. Do you think they feel living in Japan is convenient?

   B: ❶Honestly speaking, I don't think so. I think that one of the biggest difficulties they have is language. Japanese is totally different from any other language. I guess it's not easy for them to learn it.

   A: ❷I feel the same way. ❸Besides that, there are local rules such as how to throw away trash. Living in Japan means that they need to learn how to follow these local rules even if the rules are different from their home culture.

• *Example 2:*

   A: Do you think Japan is convenient for foreign residents to work and live?

   B: I agree with this idea. Japan has a reputation of having a mostly stable economy. This means that it is a good place to work. According to the Immigration Bureau, in 2018, there were more than 2.6 million foreign residents in Japan and the number is increasing every year.

   A: That's a big number, ❹but even so, I take the opposite stance. ❺Take technical interns for example. Many of them are low-wage workers. I don't think they feel that Japan is so convenient.

2. In the same conversation, if you find any evidence from an outside source, highlight it.

Step 3. This time, take a different stance from your partner and do a little research. Find more evidence and write a dialogue with your partner.

Step 4. Read the dialogue aloud with your partner.

Step 5. Then, try to come to a conclusion. Whether you come to the same conclusions or not, write the reason why.

Example

- **We reached the same conclusion. Both of us agree with the statement mainly because···**

- **We did not reach the same conclusion. One agrees with the statement mainly because···, and the other disagrees with it mainly because···**

Step 6. Next, form a new group with three other students and have a new discussion about your ideas. You are free to take either side and use any evidence you used in Step 3.

Research Presentation and Writing

Find your own topics for a research presentation or writing related to the unit's theme, or use one of the ones from below:

1. The kinds of foreign residential status in Japan
2. Cities that have the most foreign residents in Japan
3. Japanese classes given to foreign residents

Education: Online Learning

Introduction

CD 1-58

A **Listen to the following news story and fill in the blanks.**

Rika Kihira is a famous figure skater. She entered N High School in 2018. It is a "net high school," where students engage in ¹( ) learning and don't have to go to school every day like ²( ) high school students. The high school was established in 2016 by Kadokawa, which sells a range of digitized content, and Dwango, which is an internet-based entertainment enterprise. At her 5 school, students often study ³( ), watching videos at home, or wherever they happen to be, even ⁴( ). They can choose how many days they go to school in a week or in a year. Many of them study the basic ⁵( ) such as math and science online and go to school to learn more hands-on ⁶( ) such as programming, ⁷( ), and designing, according to 10 their ⁸( ). In 2018, there were nearly ⁹( ) thousand students attending distance learning high schools in Japan. This means that one in ¹⁰( ) high school students chose this style of learning.

B **The following are key phrases for the topic. Look them up in your dictionary and write the meanings.**

1. distance learning _____
2. study the basic subjects _____
3. learn hands-on skills _____
4. a computer and a headset _____
5. control "big data" _____
6. adaptive learning _____

C **What do you see in these pictures? Talk about it with your partner.**

1.

2.

3.

Education should be given equally to all children. Therefore, in many countries, there is a national curriculum that schools need to follow, so what children learn is already decided. For example, all children learn multiplication in math more or less at the same age at school. Moreover, there are common timetables throughout the
5 year which tell children when to go to school and which subjects they learn on a particular day of the week. However, some parents wonder whether all children have to attend school the same way using the same curriculum. This is because children learn differently. They have their own learning style and learning pace.

It is extremely difficult for teachers to teach children according to their
10 learning styles. This is because in order to do so, they would have to teach students individually using separate materials. However, technology offers teachers a wide choice of how they can teach. To begin with, AI, artificial intelligence, can tell teachers the most suitable level and speed for each child. Moreover, online video classes allow children to take lessons separately with a computer and a headset,
15 anywhere and anytime. Furthermore, VR, virtual reality, can make children feel as if they were experiencing activities themselves. 5G, fifth-generation mobile network, can connect these online devices quickly and stably. For example, children can talk with peers and teachers from their homes as if they were in the same room.

The role of schools and teachers has changed dramatically since the fourth
20 industrial revolution. Now AI systems control "big data." They can find the best study curriculum for each student from a huge store of data. Thus, adaptive learning software has been developed. The software can work differently for each student by adjusting questions according to their level of understanding. In this way, teaching can be adapted to learners, rather than learners trying to adapt themselves to the
25 traditional teaching style. It is time educators thought about what "equal education" means to individual children.

A Read the passage and answer the questions .

1. What is the question some parents have about education?

_____

2. How can technology be used in education?

_____

3. How is adaptive learning useful for children?

_____

B Complete an outline of the reading passage

I. Education in most countries

    A. What is common in most countries

        1. The _____ tells teachers what and when to teach.

        2. The _____ tells children when and what they learn.

    B. A question from some parents

        1. Do children have to study the _____ way?

        2. Reasons for the question

            a. Each child has his/her own _____ of learning.

            b. Each child has his/her own _____ of learning.

II. A wide choice of teaching offered by technology

    A. AI can identify the most _____ level and speed of a child.

    B. Online video classes allow children to study _____ and

        _____ .

    C. VR can give _____ experience to children.

    D. 5G can connect online devices _____ and _____ .

III. The role of schools and teachers after the fourth industrial revolution

    A. AI systems control "big data."

        1. AI can find the best _____ for each student.

        2. Adaptive learning software has been developed.

        3. The system can _____ questions according to the student's level.

    B. Teaching can be _____ to learners' learning style or level.

Data

A Study the figure and fill in the blanks.

 1-62

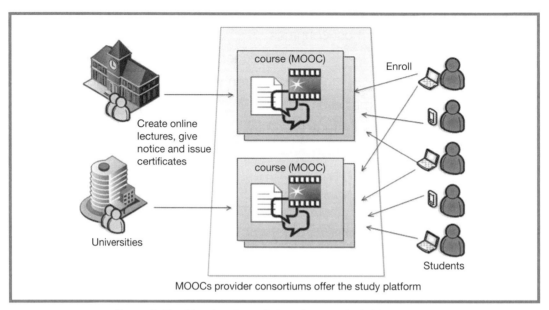

Figure 1: The Massive Open Online Courses (MOOCs) system

Source: オージス総研 「広がる大規模公開オンライン講座 MOOC」より作成
https://www.ogis-ri.co.jp/rad/webmaga/rwm20141001.html

Figure 1 shows the system of MOOCs, which stands for the "¹( )
( ) ( ) ( )". The system aims to give college online
courses freely to anyone. The MOOCs ²( ) ( ), which
are groups of various educational organizations, offer the study ³( ).
5 A platform is a system on the website. People can choose and ⁴( )
in any course from this platform online. One example of a consortium is edX,
which includes Harvard University and MIT. Japanese universities such as Kyoto
University and the University of Tokyo are also members of edX. Most of the
courses are taught in English. In this way, people can take lectures given by some
10 of the best universities in the world at home. When a student finishes a course, a
⁵( ) can be issued depending on the course. Students can even get
a college degree if they finish the required courses. Because MOOCs offer free
online video lectures, students can study in any ⁶( ) in the world and
at any ⁷( ) of the day without paying ⁸( ). The only thing students
15 need is a computer or a smartphone connected to the Internet. The courses also
offer open chatrooms and give prompt feedback to students so that they can learn
interactively with others.

NOTES

enroll 入学手続きをする　MIT (Massachusetts Institute of Technology) マサチューセッツ工科大学
certificate 証書　prompt 迅速な

B Study the figure and fill in the blanks.

 1-63

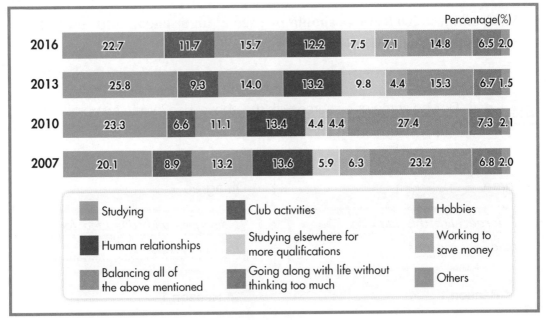

Figure 2: Most important thing in college life

Source: 溝上慎一 「大学生白書 2018 いまの大学教育では学生を変えられない」より作成

A: The figure shows how Japanese college students think about their college life. A survey asked 2,000 college students what the most important thing was in their college life. The survey was conducted once every three years from [1](   ) to [2](   ). So, what do you think is the most important thing in your college life? Is it studying, hobbies, or something else?   5

B: Well, for me, it's club activities, but the most recent result in the figure shows that [3](   ) was the most important thing. [4](   ) percent of the respondents gave this answer in 2016. How about you?

A: I would say human relationships because I think friends are important. In 2016, the second most common answer was [5](   ) and 10 human relationships came in third. Having said that, it seems that a lot of students couldn't choose which because 14.8 percent of them answered [6](   ) all of the most important things mentioned here.

B: Hmm. It's interesting to see that the biggest change over the nine years was that students who gave that answer decreased from [7](   ) percent to 14.8 15 percent. This means that college students have become clearer about what they want to put weight on.

NOTES

qualification 資格 respondent 回答者

Discussion

A Agree or disagree?

> **More online video lectures should be used at high schools and colleges so that students can study at their own pace.**

Step 1. Do you agree or disagree with the above idea? Write two or three reasons supporting each side.

Agree

> I agree with this idea for the following reasons:

✓ Reason 1

....
....
....
....

✓ Reason 2

....
....
....
....

✓ Reason 3

....
....
....
....

Disagree

> I disagree with this idea for the following reasons:

✓ Reason 1

....
....
....
....

✓ Reason 2

....
....
....
....

✓ Reason 3

....
....
....
....

Step 2. Learn the discussion strategies.

 1-64、65

1. In pairs, read out the following conversation. Write the numbers of the underlined expressions in the appropriate discussion strategies below.

Agreeing ____

Hypothesizing ____

Saying in different words ____

Making a positive point ____

Asking for more explanations ____

- *Example 1:*

  A: What do you think about using online video lectures at schools?

  B: I agree with it because we can learn at our own pace. The good thing is that we can rewind the video if we didn't understand clearly.

  A: ❶<u>That makes sense</u>. We can watch the lecture as many times as we like. But, I disagree with this idea because it's fun to learn with others. ❷<u>What I mean is that</u> we can share ideas and learn how to build good relationships.

- *Example 2:*

  A: What do you think about the use of online video lectures at schools?

  B: I agree with it because we can use our time effectively. ❸<u>Imagine how our life may change if</u> we start taking online lectures.

  A: That's right. ❹<u>It must be</u> a big change. According to the Ministry of Education, Culture, Sports, Science and Technology, about one in 20 high school students went to distance learning schools in 2018. ❺<u>It will also be a big advantage for</u> students who work.

  B: ❻<u>Can you tell me more</u>?

2. In the same conversation, if you find any evidence from an outside source, highlight it.

Step 3. This time, take a different stance from your partner and do a little research. Find more evidence and write a dialogue with your partner.

Step 4. Read the dialogue aloud with your partner.

Step 5. Then, try to come to a conclusion. Whether you come to the same conclusions or not, write the reason why.

Example

- **We reached the same conclusion. Both of us agree with the statement mainly because···**

- **We did not reach the same conclusion. One agrees with the statement mainly because···, and the other disagrees with it mainly because···**

Step 6. Next, form a new group with three other students and have a new discussion about your ideas. You are free to take either side and use any evidence you used in Step 3.

Research Presentation and Writing

Find your own topics for a research presentation or writing related to the unit's theme, or use one of the ones from below:

1. Computer programing taught as compulsory education
2. The theory of multiple intelligences
3. Examples of adaptive learning software

Culture: Entertainment

A Listen to the following news story and fill in the blanks.

"You can ¹( ), shout, or ²( ) your hands. You can "cosplay," but we have no changing room. You can use tambourines, bells, chemical ³( ), and pen sticks." These are some of the ⁴( ) a theater in Osaka gave when it showed *Bohemian Rhapsody*, a film based on the life and ⁵( ) of Freddie Mercury, the lead singer of the British rock group, 5 Queen. This example shows how more and more movie theaters are allowing their customers to ⁶( ) in the movie while watching it. Another example is *Baahubali*, a movie series from India. In the theater, you can find the ⁷( ) waving lights and ⁸( ) "Baahubali, Baahubali!" They are trying to cheer on the prince named Baahubali when he faces difficulties in the 10 ⁹( )-minute film. There are still not many theaters which allow people to act this way, but the audience might enjoy a film more if they can cheer or sing along rather than just watch it in ¹⁰( ).

B The following are key phrases for the topic. Look them up in your dictionary and write the meanings.

1. you can "cosplay" _____
2. concerts are held simultaneously _____
3. spend leisure time _____
4. get acquainted with somebody _____
5. show the festival in real time _____
6. an activity shared with others _____

C What do you see in these pictures? Talk about it with your partner.

1.
2.
3.

Going to theaters, amusement parks and festivals are some popular ways to spend your free time. At theaters, people usually sit quietly and watch the performance, while at amusement parks and festivals, people usually walk around from one attraction to another. However, more people are now keen to participate more

5 actively. One example is what they do when they attend live performances.

The way people behave at pop music concerts in Japan has been changing since the late 1990s when rock festivals began to be held. According to Professor Junichi Nagai of Kobe Yamate University, people go to rock festivals for various reasons. First, they enjoy the atmosphere. The festivals are often held outside cities, where

10 people can enjoy nature. Some offer camping facilities so that people can stay overnight. Second, people go to rock festivals to talk with friends. Concerts are held simultaneously at different stages. People can plan how much time they spend at different stages and how much time they spend chatting with their friends. Another reason is that they can get acquainted with new groups of people. Some of them

15 become "festival buddies (fesu-nakama)" and visit other festivals together. Social media can connect these people over time. These reasons show that people not only enjoy the live performances but also value the time spent with others.

Technology is also changing the way people take part in events in their free time. Niconico Chokaigi is an annual festival held at Makuhari Messe featuring video

20 games, anime and cosplay. In 2019, more than 161,000 people visited the venue and more than 6 million people visited the online video site, which showed the festival in real time. The comments of online visitors are shared continuously in real time, too. They are displayed on the big screen at the venue, so that all the participants can connect with each other no matter where they are. Activities shared with others are

25 also valued here.

A Read the passage and answer the questions .

1. What do people usually do at theaters, amusement parks and festivals?

_____

2. Why do people go to rock festivals?

_____

3. How has technology made Niconico Chokaigi unique?

_____

B Complete an outline of the reading passage.

I. Attitudes of people at theaters, amusement parks and festivals
    A. General attitudes
        1. People sit _____ and watch performances.
        2. People walk around from one attraction to another.
    B. Recent attitudes seen
        1. People have a desire to _____ more actively.
        2. One example is what people do when they attend live performances.

II. The emergence of rock festivals
    A. Began in the late _____
    B. Reasons for going to rock festivals by Professor Junichi Nagai
        1. People enjoy the _____.
        2. People _____ with friends.
        3. People get _____ with new groups of people.
    C. People _____ the time spent with others.

III. How technology affects people's attitudes
    A. At Niconico Chokaigi
        1. More than 6 million people visited the _____ video site.
        2. They watched the festival in _____ time.
        3. _____ are shown on the screen.
        4. All the visitors can connect with each other.
    B. People value activities _____ with others.

A Study the figure and fill in the blanks.

 2-05

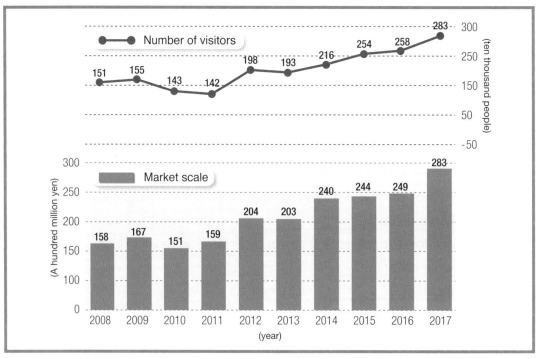

Figure 1: Number of visitors and market scale of music festivals in Japan

Source: ぴあ総研 「多様化が進み、活況が続く音楽フェスの市場動向／ぴあ総研が調査結果を公表」より作成
https://corporate.pia.jp/news/detail_live_enta 201808_fes.html

Figure 1 shows the number of visitors and the market scale of music festivals in Japan from [1](   ) to [2](   ). The festivals include two of the biggest rock festivals in Japan, which are Fuji Rock, first held in 1997, and Rock in Japan first held in 2000. They are held in Niigata Prefecture and Ibaraki

5 Prefecture, respectively. These are just a few of the rock festivals held in Japan. The [3](   ) vertical axis shows the number of people in units of 10,000 and the [4](   ) vertical axis, the market scale in units of 100 million yen. The number of people attending music festivals has increased gradually since 2008. Over 9 years, the number increased by more than [5](   ) million from about 1.5 million to 2.8

10 million. This is an increase of more than [6](   ) percent. The market scale also expanded from [7](   ) billion yen to [8](   ) billion yen, which means that the market size rose by as much as 12.5 billion yen. This figure includes [9](   ) sales. For example, a one-day ticket will cost about 20,000 yen for Fuji Rock and 14,000 yen for Rock in Japan. More than 50 artists perform in each

15 festival in one day.

NOTES

market scale 市場規模　vertical axis 縦軸　gradually ゆっくりと　expand 拡大する

B Study the figure and fill in the blanks.

 2-06

Figure 2: Comments on Cho Kabuki posted on a live video

Source: 「ニコニコ超会議 2018 超歌舞伎」より作成

A: This picture describes a scene displayed on a screen at the venue of Cho Kabuki in 2018. It's a special kabuki performance held every year featuring a vocaloid named [1](   ), and Shido Nakamura, a famous kabuki [2](   ).

B: Did you say vocaloid? What exactly is it?   5

A: The word is a mix of "[3](   )" and "[4](   )". It's voice synthesizer software that creates digital voices.

B: Hmm. Sounds very new to me. This must be a new type of kabuki, quite different from the original one. Say, what are these numbers and words displayed?   10

A: They are a kind of [5](   ), or *kakegoe* in Japanese. They are posted by people viewing on the [6](   ). Their words appear instantly on the big screen next to the stage during the performance. The chain of number "[7](   )" represents the sound of clapping [8](   ), or *pachi-pachi-pachi* in Japanese.   15

B: What about the word, "*dashi* (出汁)", soup stock, displayed on the left side?

A: It's a homophone of "*dashi* (山車)", a float in festivals, which vehicle Miku is riding on. People are playing with words, too.

B: I see. I heard that *kakegoe* is an essential element of a kabuki performance to [9](   ) actors. I also heard that women are not allowed to shout like 20 this. However if it's an Internet post, women can also do it.

NOTES

venue 会場　vocal 声の　android アンドロイド（人造人間）　instantly すぐに
essential きわめて重要な　Internet post インターネットからの投稿

A Agree or disagree?

> **The entertainment industry should offer customers more opportunities to play an active role in events to create greater customer satisfaction.**

Step 1. <u>Do you agree or disagree with the above idea?</u> Write two or three reasons supporting each side.

Agree	Disagree
I agree with this idea for the following reasons	*I disagree with this idea for the following reasons:*

✓ Reason 1

....
....
....
....

✓ Reason 1

....
....
....
....

✓ Reason 2

....
....
....
....

✓ Reason 2

....
....
....
....

✓ Reason 3

....
....
....
....

✓ Reason 3

....
....
....
....

Step 2. Learn the discussion strategies.

 2-07、08

1. In pairs, read out the following conversation. Write the numbers of the underlined expressions in the appropriate discussion strategies below.

Asking for more explanations ____   Comparing and contrasting ____

Saying in different words ____   Disagreeing ____

Agreeing ____

• *Example 1:*

A: Nowadays, the entertainment industry gives customers the chance to play an active role. What do you think about that?

B: I agree with it because this will add more value.

A: What do you mean?

B: ❶Let me put it into other words. ❷In the past, people were just entertained and were satisfied with it, but the situation is different now. We need more satisfaction.

A: ❸Could you be more specific?

B: For example, chanting together at movie theaters like the theaters which showed *Bohemian Rhapsody* and *Baahubali*.

• *Example 2:*

A: If you were in the entertainment business, would you try to increase customer satisfaction by allowing people to participate more in events?

B: ❹I completely agree. Niconico Chokaigi 2019 reported that more than 6 million people visited the net video site. They participated by posting comments.

A: That's a big number, ❺but I don't think I can agree with you. Some people may like to be a passive observer and enjoy an event quietly.

2. In the same conversation, if you find any evidence from an outside source, highlight it.

Step 3. This time, take a different stance from your partner and do a little research. Find more evidence and write a dialogue with your partner.

Step 4. Read the dialogue aloud with your partner.

Step 5. Then, try to come to a conclusion. Whether you come to the same conclusions or not, write the reason why.

Example

- **We reached the same conclusion. Both of us agree with the statement mainly because…**

- **We did not reach the same conclusion. One agrees with the statement mainly because…, and the other disagrees with it mainly because…**

Step 6. Next, form a new group with three other students and have a new discussion about your ideas. You are free to take either side and use any evidence you used in Step 3.

Research Presentation and Writing

Find your own topics for a research presentation or writing related to the unit's theme, or use one of the ones from below:

1. Cosplay culture in Japan and overseas
2. Types of vocaloids used in various fields
3. Making young people interested in kabuki

UNIT 10

Science:
The New Agricultural Revolution

Introduction

CD 2-09

A Listen to the following news story and fill in the blanks.

Can you tell me which tomatoes at a supermarket are the most delicious? Sure!
They should be [1](   ) red, the ring of small [2](   ) at the end
should be fresh and green, and there should also be white, [3](   )
lines at the top. In other words, there are some common [4](   ).
Recently, however, AI can describe the taste of each tomato. Right after some 5
[5](   ) of the tomatoes are taken, a pentagon-shaped graph appears on
a screen and shows how high each tomato rates on five points: [6](   ),
bitterness, flavor/umami, [7](   ), and sweetness. This is accompanied
by a short comment such as, "This tomato tastes a little bitter, but has a strong
flavor." AI uses the three [8](   ) colors of light called "RGB"(red-green-blue). 10
It also recognizes more colors behind the top-level RGB, and describes the taste
based on big data of more than [9](   ) pieces of information. By using this
system, AI can now predict the taste of 16 different fruits and vegetables.

B The following are key phrases for the topic. Look them up in your dictionary and write the meanings.

1. describe the taste of tomatoes   _____
2. is based on big data   _____
3. is at risk   _____
4. increases efficiency in growing crops   _____
5. smart agriculture   _____

C What do you see in these pictures? Talk about it with your partner.

1.
2.
3.

Agriculture in Japan is at risk. During the past three decades, farmland has decreased by 16 percent, total agricultural production has decreased by 19 percent, and the food self-sufficiency rate fell from 48 percent to 38 percent. Also, the farming population has dropped from 4.8 million to 1.7 million. It will drop even further

5 because many farmers are getting old. Although many restaurants try to use meat and vegetables produced in Japan, Japanese farmers cannot keep up with the demand. As a result, some of those restaurants have to use imported products. However, we are seeing great developments in technology, and there is hope that they will save Japanese agriculture.

10 The Internet of Things (IoT) collects big data, artificial intelligence (AI) analyzes it and creates know-how. IoT is the infrastructure of interconnected objects, people, system, and information resources. In agriculture, these technologies help to increase the efficiency of growing crops, and to reform the way farmers work. They can be applied to two major fields of agriculture: farm machines, such as drones and tractors,

15 and a distribution system such as online wholesale markets. These developments involve various organizations, including small and medium-sized IT startups, farm machinery manufacturers, communication companies, universities, and even the Japanese government.

The food technologies are gene-editing and genetically modified organisms

20 (GMOs). Gene-editing can remove an existing gene from plants or animals. For example, it can remove a horn gene to produce a hornless cow. This can help prevent injuries without having to physically remove a horn. Examples being developed in Japan are potatoes without toxins, larger fish, and tomatoes that can lower blood pressure. GMOs use genes from one organism and insert them into others. For

25 example, Bt corn has a gene inserted from a bacterium which produces a protein that is toxic to certain insects. Most scientists say these foods are safe to eat, but many people have strong doubts that they truly are.

A Read the passage and answer the questions.

1. Why is Japanese agriculture at risk?

_____

2. What kinds of organizations are involved with development?

_____

3. What is the difference between gene-editing and GMOs?

_____

B Complete an outline of the reading passage.

I. Agriculture in Japan is at risk.

    A. Farmland has decreased by 16 percent.

    B. Total production has decreased _____.

    C. The food self-sufficiency rate fell to _____.

    D. The farming _____ has dropped from 4.8 to 1.7 million.

    E. Farmers cannot keep up with demand.

II. IoT, Big Data, and AI in agriculture

    A. Purposes:

        1. to increase the _____ of growing crops

        2. to reform the way _____

    B. Applied to two major technological fields of agriculture:

        1. farm machines: _____ and tractors

        2. a distribution system: _____ wholesale markets

III. Two types of food technologies

    A. gene-editing

        1. to _____ an existing gene from plants or animals

            a. a hornless cow

    B. _____

        1. Genes from one organism are inserted into others.

            a. Bt corn

Data

A Study the figure and fill in the blanks.

 2-13

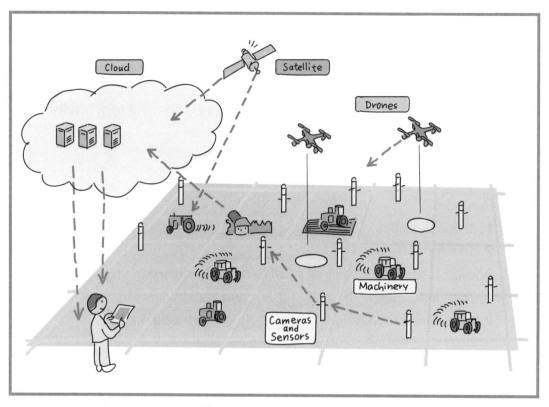

Figure 1: Smart Agriculture

Source: 窪田新之助『日本発「ロボットAI農業」の凄い未来』より作成

    Figure 1 shows an image of smart agriculture or "Agri-Tech." ¹(   ) are flying over the field to monitor growth status, spot harmful insects, and spread fertilizer with pinpoint accuracy, even during the night, by using deep-learning. Deep learning refers to machine learning techniques that enable machines to learn
5 features and tasks from several layers of data such as images, text, and sound. Additionally, drones can hang a light trap for catching moths, work as night-vision, and act as thermo-cameras. On the ground, there are unmanned ²(   ) to cultivate land and harvest crops. Three or even four robot tractors can operate ³(   ), and turn around a few seconds apart from each other. Farmers
10 can control them from a hand-held ⁴(   ). There are also many poles in the field equipped with cameras and field ⁵(   ). They gather information about outdoor temperature, soil temperature, soil moisture, and solar radiation. Furthermore, they transmit this data to ⁶(   ) servers.

NOTES

growth status 成長状態　harmful insects 害虫　fertilizer 化学肥料　features 特徴　layers 層
light trap 明かりのわな　unmanned 無人の　hand-held 手に持った　poles 棒・柱
solar radiation 太陽放射

B Study the figure and fill in the blanks.

 2-14

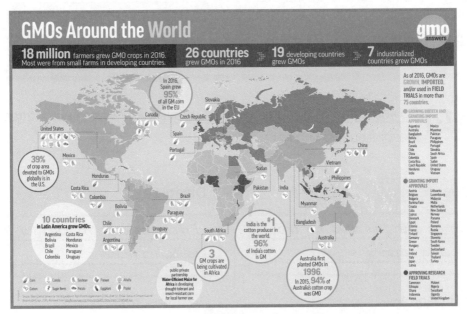

Figure 2: GMOs Around the World

Source: GMOanswers "GMOs Globally." Data from ISAAA.
(The International Service for the Acquisition of Agri-biotech Applications) https://gmoanswers.com/gmos-globally

A: Figure 2 shows the status of GMOs around the world. It says [1](   ) million farmers in [2](   ) countries grew GMO crops in 2016, and 19 of them were [3](   ) countries, while seven were industrialized countries.

B: I know that the top five countries growing GMO crops were the U.S., Brazil, Argentina, Canada, and India.   5

A: The United States is the largest producer, planting [4](   ) percent of total global production. In 2016, American farmers grew GMO corn, cotton, soybeans, canola, sugar beets, alfalfa, papaya, potatoes, and summer squash on over 728,280 km^2. This is about twice the area of Japan.

B: Speaking about Japan, we don't grow many GMO crops and mostly 10 [5](   ) them. I heard that the opposition to GMO foods runs especially strong in Japan. Putting that aside for now, however, if GMOs increase food productivity, the countries in [6](   ) should grow them because some of them are suffering from severe hunger.

A: That's right. Actually, South Africa is one of the top ten developing countries to 15 plant GMO crops, and many other countries in the gray zone have conducted field trials and research on crops with special traits related to drought-tolerance and high nutrient content.

NOTES

industrialized 工業化した canola カノラ（植物）sugar beets テンサイ productivity 生産性
traits 特性 drought-tolerance 耐乾性 nutrient 栄養

Discussion

A Agree or disagree?

> **Japan should grow GMO crops.**

Step 1. Do you agree or disagree with the above idea? Write two or three reasons supporting each side.

Agree

> I agree with this idea for the following reasons.

✓ **Reason 1**

....
....
....
....

✓ **Reason 2**

....
....
....
....

✓ **Reason 3**

....
....
....
....

Disagree

> I disagree with this idea for the following reasons.

✓ **Reason 1**

....
....
....
....

✓ **Reason2**

....
....
....
....

✓ **Reason 3**

....
....
....
....

Step 2. Learn the discussion strategies.

2-15、16

1. In pairs, read out the following conversation. Write the numbers of the underlined expressions in the appropriate discussion strategies below.

Agreeing ____   Asking for an opinion ____

Disagreeing ____   Referring to a source ____

• *Example 1:*

A: Today, we're going to discuss whether Japan should grow GMO crops.

B: ❶I support this idea because GMO crops are already being grown all over the world ❷as the GMO Answers showed.

A: ❸That's just what I thought. And many scientists say they are safe to eat.

B: Moreover, Japan already imports them, so why not grow them here?

• *Example 2:*

A: ❹Could I have your opinion about this statement that Japan should grow GMO crops?

B: ❺I'm opposed to it because some GMO crops can have the trait of insect-resistance. If we eat them, we don't know what they will do to our bodies.

A: ❻Sorry, but I don't agree with your thinking. Scientists have shown they are safe.

B: Okay, but no one can guarantee they are safe because there might be a sudden change of structure that could be harmful.

2. In the same conversation, if you find any evidence from an outside source, highlight it.

Step 3. This time, take a different stance from your partner and do a little research. Find more evidence and write a dialogue with your partner.

Step 4. Read the dialogue aloud with your partner.

Step 5. Then, try to come to a conclusion. Whether you come to the same conclusions or not, write the reason why.

Example

- **We reached the same conclusion. Both of us agree with the statement mainly because…**

- **We did not reach the same conclusion. One agrees with the statement mainly because…, and the other disagrees with it mainly because…**

Step 6. Next, form a new group with three other students and have a new discussion about your ideas. You are free to take either side and use any evidence you used in Step 3.

Research Presentation and Writing

Find your own topics for a research presentation or writing related to the unit's theme, or use one of the ones from below:

1. Other technologies in agriculture
2. Research done by companies and universities in Japan
3. The current state of gene-editing and GMO foods in Japan
4. Research on the effects of GMO foods on human health

UNIT 11

The Aging Society: Elderly Drivers

A **Listen to the following news story and fill in the blanks.**

An ¹( )-year-old man was arrested ²( ) for hitting two high school students with his car in Gunma Prefecture, after first damaging a car driving in the ³( ) lane, police said. The two were hit in the city of Maebashi, at around ⁴( ) a.m., leaving one ⁵( ) and the other ⁶( ) ⁷( ). They were on their way to school by bicycle. "The accident happened before I realized," the driver said. The police said there was no sign that he had used his ⁸( ). Recently, his family had asked him to give up driving because he had already ⁹( ) a minor accident.

B **The following are key phrases for the topic. Look them up in your dictionary and write the meanings.**

1. have /cause a traffic accident _____
2. people aged 75 or older _____
3. no sign of using the brakes _____
4. accidentally press/hit the gas pedal instead of the brakes

   _____
5. give up their driver's licenses _____
6. have a cognitive function test _____
7. show signs of dementia _____

C **What do you see in these pictures? Talk about it with your partner.**

93

The percentage of fatal traffic accidents caused by people 75 years old or older has increased in Japan. According to the National Police Agency (NPA), it rose from 7.4 percent in 2005 to 12.9 percent in 2017. There were 418 out of 3,247 cases in 2017, and 49 percent of the elderly drivers who caused fatal accidents showed some

5 signs of dementia or lowered cognitive abilities. If accidents included damaging objects or buildings, the percentage of traffic accidents caused by such drivers would be even higher. As Japan's population continues to age, these accidents will become a major problem.

The Road Traffic Law requires that elderly people take a cognitive function test

10 every three years when they renew their driver's licenses. A medical checkup is then required if any signs of dementia are found, and their driver's licenses will be officially taken away. Doctors are also asked to report to the public safety commission in each prefecture if any of their patients who drive suffer from dementia. However, stricter laws alone cannot make elderly people stop driving because some need cars

15 for daily activities such as shopping and going to the doctor. Also, their physical abilities may have weakened only slightly.

We need to think about how to support these people and how to prevent accidents. In Saga City, for example, volunteers living in the city created a system to offer alternative transportation to elderly people who give up their driver's licenses. The

20 system is financed by donations and *furusatonozei*, a hometown tax. The NPA also plans to introduce a "limited" driver's license. Some elderly people are only allowed to drive with automatic brakes and a vision enhancement system, for example. Or, as in Victoria, Australia, some of them can only drive during the daytime, or to go to the supermarket or the doctor.

A Read the passage and answer the questions.

1. In 2017, there were 418 fatal accidents involving elderly drivers. Why is this becoming a major problem?

_____

2. How can we detect elderly drivers who suffer from dementia?

_____

3. What is a "limited" driver's license?

_____

B Complete an outline of the reading passage.

I. The increase in fatal traffic accidents by people 75 or older

    A. From 7.4% in 2005 to _____

    B. 49% of the elderly drivers – some signs of _____ or lower _____ abilities

    C. More accidents if it includes damaging objects or buildings

    D. It will become a _____ with the aging society.

II. The _____ Law

    A. It requires elderly people to:

        1. renew their licenses every _____.

        2. take a _____ test when they renew their driver's licenses.

        3. get a _____ checkup if they show _____.

    B. It asks a doctor to:

    report to the public _____ commission if they find any of their patients who suffer from dementia.

    C. It alone cannot make elderly people stop driving because:

        1. some need cars for daily activities such as _____ and _____.

        2. their _____ abilities may have weakened only _____.

III. Support systems

    A. A system to offer alternative _____:

        1. In Saga, volunteers created the system.

        2. Their financial sources: donations and _____

    B. The NPA plans to introduce _____.

        1. Some are allowed to drive only with automatic _____.

        2. Some are allowed to drive only during _____.

        3. Some are allowed to drive only to go to the supermarket or _____.

A Study the figure and fill in the blanks.

 2-21

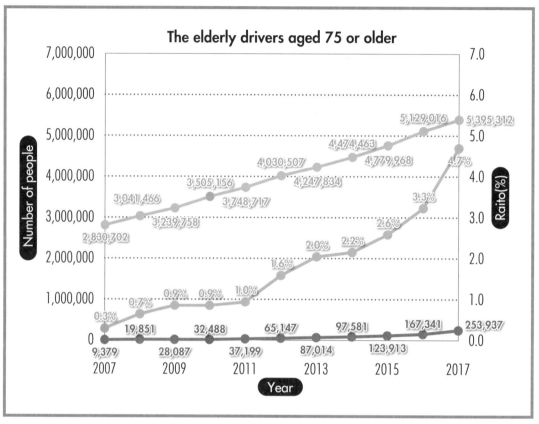

Figure 1: Elderly drivers age 75 or older

Source: 警察庁運転免許統計より作成
https://www.npa.go.jp/publications/statistics/koutsuu/menkyo.html

Figure 1 shows the changes in elderly drivers aged 75 or older. The blue line shows the number of elderly drivers, the red line shows the number of such drivers who voluntarily returned their licenses, and the green line shows the ratio. The left vertical axis shows the population of elderly drivers and the horizontal axis shows

5 the years from [1](   ) to [2](   ). The total number of elderly drivers reached [3](   ) in 2017, and [4](   ) people returned their licenses voluntarily. In 2007, [5](   ) people returned their licenses, and the ratio was only [6](   ) percent. From 2016 to 2017, the increase was sharp; however, it accounted for only [7](   ) percent of elderly drivers as a whole.

NOTES

voluntarily 自発的に   account for 占める

B Look at the figure and fill in the blanks.

 2-22

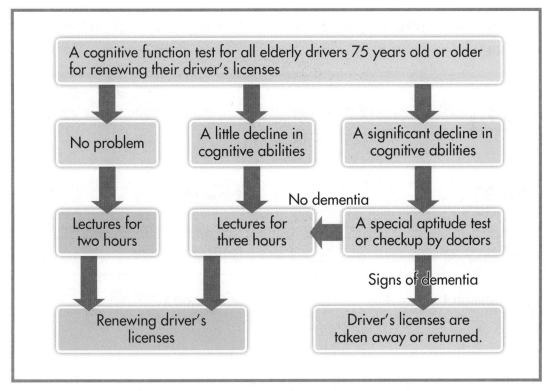

A cognitive function test for all elderly drivers 75 years old or older for renewing their driver's licenses

No problem

A little decline in cognitive abilities

A significant decline in cognitive abilities

No dementia

Lectures for two hours

Lectures for three hours

A special aptitude test or checkup by doctors

Signs of dementia

Renewing driver's licenses

Driver's licenses are taken away or returned.

Figure 2: the system of renewing driver's licenses for elderly drivers

Source: 警察庁 (National Police Agency)「認知機能検査について」より作成
https://www.npa.go.jp/policies/application/license_renewal/ninchi.html

A: Figure 2 shows the system for detecting elderly drivers with [1]( ).

B: Oh, I know a little about this because my 78-year-old grandmother took a test recently. She seemed to be showing a decline in her cognitive abilities, but she passed a [2]( ) [3]( ) [4]( ).

A: How did your family feel about it? 5

B: Oh, we're very worried about her. Although she insists that she needs to drive every day, we're really afraid that she may cause an accident or kill someone. Having lectures for [5]( ) [6]( ) doesn't guarantee anything.

A: I know what you mean. People like her must be the most difficult to deal with. They don't show any signs of [7]( ), so their driver's licenses are not 10 [8]( ) away.

NOTES

a cognitive function test 認知機能検査　a special aptitude test 臨時適性検査　guarantee 保証する

Discussion

A Agree or disagree?

> **We should require everyone aged 75 or older to give up their driver's license.**

Step 1. <u>Do you agree or disagree with the above idea?</u> Write two or three reasons supporting each side.

Agree	Disagree
I agree with this idea for the following reasons.	*I disagree with this idea for the following reasons.*

✓ Reason 1

....
....
....
....

✓ Reason 2

....
....
....
....

✓ Reason 3

....
....
....
....

✓ Reason 1

....
....
....
....

✓ Reason 2

....
....
....
....

✓ Reason 3

....
....
....
....

Step 2. Learn the discussion strategies.   2-23, 24

1. In pairs, read out the following conversation. Write the numbers of the underlined expressions in the appropriate discussion strategies below.

Agreeing ____   Giving your opinion ____

Disagreeing ____   Asking for more explanation ____

Not sure ____   Referring to a source ____

• *Example 1:*

> A: Would you agree with this proposal? Actually, ❶in my view, this is a good idea because elderly drivers have caused a lot of accidents recently.

> B: ❷You've got that right. ❸According to the NPA, they were involved in 460 accidents, which makes up 15 percent of the entire number of fatal car and bike accidents.

> A: That's clearly true. We just have to take steps to prevent it before any accidents happen.

• *Example 2:*

> A: ❹I'm opposed to this proposal because some elderly people cannot live without cars.

> B: ❺I'm not so sure about that. ❻Could you give me an example?

> A: For example, think about people who live in the country. They don't have enough public transportation for daily shopping.

> B: I guess so, but there might be another way for rural residents to buy things these days.

2. In the same conversation, if you find any evidence from an outside source, highlight it.

Step 3. This time, take a different stance from your partner and do a little research. Find more evidence and write a dialogue with your partner.

Step 4. Read the dialogue aloud with your partner.

Step 5. Then, try to come to a conclusion. Whether you come to the same conclusions or not, write the reason why.

Example

- **We reached the same conclusion. Both of us agree with the statement mainly because…**

- **We did not reach the same conclusion. One agrees with the statement mainly because…, and the other disagrees with it mainly because…**

Step 6. Next, form a new group with three other students and have a new discussion about your ideas. You are free to take either side and use any evidence you used in Step 3.

Research Presentation and Writing

Find your own topics for a research presentation or writing related to the unit's theme, or use one of the ones from below:

1. Recent news about traffic accidents caused by elderly drivers
2. Measures to persuade the elderly to return their driver's licenses
3. Situation in other countries

UNIT 12

DNA: Advances in DNA Technology

Introduction

 2-25

A Listen to the following news story and fill in the blanks.

For the first time in the world, a ¹(   ) scientist claimed he had succeeded in creating gene-edited babies. He said that he changed the DNA of ²(   ) because their father was ³(   ) with HIV. The DNA of the twins needed to become ⁴(   ) to the HIV virus. Furthermore, he revealed there was another woman taking part in his research who was still pregnant with gene-edited ⁵ eggs. Right after his announcement, China's government ordered this project to be stopped, saying it was ⁵(   ) and unacceptable. Many scientists from other countries also said that this conduct was irresponsible and ⁶(   ). This procedure may affect ⁷(   ) genes of the babies by accident and could even have a ⁸(   ) effect in the future when these babies grow up ¹⁰ and have children because the risks are not yet known.

B The following are key phrases for the topic. Look them up in your dictionary and write the meanings.

1. gene-edited / edit genome   _____
2. change/ alter the DNA   _____
3. A conduct is ethical / unethical.   _____
4. initialize the DNA   _____
5. use induced pluripotent stem (iPS) cells   _____
6. identify the possibility of getting certain diseases   _____

C What do you see in these pictures? Talk about it with your partner.

1.

2.

3.
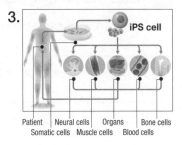

Recently, DNA technology has advanced in two ways. One way is to alter the DNA by editing the genome. "Editing" means to change an organism's DNA. This technology has been widely used with plants and animals and more recently been applied to human embryos. The other technology is to initialize the DNA and generate induced pluripotent stem (iPS) cells, created in 2007 by Professor Shinya Yamanaka of Kyoto University. Professor Yamanaka introduced four genes into ordinary human cells to differentiate into any type of cell in the body. Therefore, it is expected that iPS cells will greatly contribute to regenerative medicine.

The advancement of DNA analysis has also produced a large shift in people's mindsets. For example, some DNA tests can identify the possibility of getting certain diseases. When Angelina Jolie was diagnosed with an 87 percent chance of breast cancer and a 50 percent chance of ovarian cancer, she had preventive surgery in 2013 and 2015, respectively. Another example is that the number of women receiving prenatal genetic testing in Japan reached over 50,000 between 2013 and 2017. This test uses a blood sample from the mother and identifies the condition of the embryo.

DNA analysis has also become a part of people's daily lives. For example, a Japanese cosmetic company provides customers with DNA testing for certain physical conditions, such as where to gain more fat in your body, or the possibility to develop facial spots and wrinkles. This service is conducted using only a person's saliva. In the U.S., DNA tests have become popular as gifts. One of the company's catchphrases is, "Don't you want to find your roots?" The test costs about $100 and uses a pie chart to show a person's racial composition, such as 25 percent Italian, 20 percent Irish, or 15 percent Greek, etc. It can also reveal blood relationships in people's family tree, which can accidentally identify criminals. This has helped police to solve several "cold cases" with DNA technology.

A Read the passage and answer the following questions.

1. What are iPS cells useful for?

2. Why did Angelina Jolie have preventive operations?

3. What is an unintended result of commercial DNA tests?

B Complete an outline of the reading passage.

I. DNA technology has developed in two ways.

    A. to alter the DNA by _____ the genome: changing an organism's DNA

        1. _____ and _____

        2. recent treatment of human embryo

    B. to initialize the DNA and generate induced pluripotent stem (___) cells: created by Professor Shinya _____ of Kyoto University, who introduced four genes into ordinary human cells to differentiate into any type of cell in the body

        1. _____ medicine

II. The advancement of DNA analysis - a large shift in people's mindsets

    A. Some DNA tests identify the possibility of getting certain _____.

        1. Angelina Jolie had _____ surgery.

        2. Japanese women had _____ genetic testing.

III. DNA analysis - a part of people's daily lives

    A. a Japanese _____ company's service with DNA testing

        1. physical conditions

            a. where to gain more ___ in your body

            b. possibility to develop facial spots and _____

    B. _____ in the U.S.

        1. to find your _____

        2. to reveal _____ relationships in people's family tree

            a. accidentally identifies _____: solved several "cold cases."

A Study the figures and fill in the blanks.

 2-29

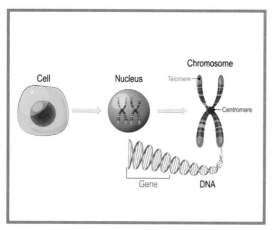

Figure 1: DNA Structure

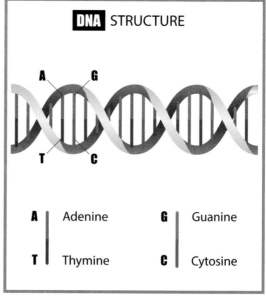

Figure 2: Deoxyribonucleic Acid (DNA)

Figure 1 shows the structure of DNA. Humans have organs made of tissues, which are made of cells, which are made of proteins. Our body contains trillions of cells, such as blood cells, bone cells, and nerve cells. There are over 200 different types of cells. How do these cells know what job to do? They get their instructions
5 from DNA. Each of these cells has a [1]( ). Human cells contain 23 pairs of [2]( ). A chromosome is made up of DNA coiled around proteins. Each piece of information is carried on a different section of the DNA. These sections are called [3]( ). They tell a cell how to make a specific protein. If we were talking about a book, DNA would be a letter, a gene would be a
10 sentence, and a chromosome would be the book itself.

DNA is short for deoxyribonucleic acid. It is a long thin molecule like a twisted ladder, made up of nucleotides. There are four types of nucleotides: adenine, thymine, cytosine, and [4]( ), which are represented by their first letters. A and [5]( ) are always bonded together, and C and [6]( ) are always bonded
15 together. The specific order of an A and T pair, and a C and G pair is what creates the unique characteristics of every person, animal, plant, and other living things.

NOTES

cells 細胞　nucleus（複数形 nuclei）核　chromosomes 染色体　nerves 神経
DNA= deoxyribonucleic acid デオキシリボ核酸（二重らせん状に　構成されている重合体）
Nucleotides ヌクレオチド（ヌクレオシドにリン酸が結合した物質）

B Study the figure and fill in the blanks

 2-30

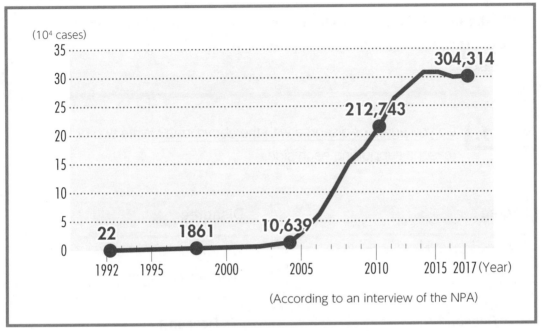

Figure 3: The number of crime cases using DNA analysis in Japan

Source: 時事ドットコムニュース「DNA 型鑑定件数の推移（2018 年 12 月）」より作成
https://www.jiji.com/jc/graphics?p=ve_soc_police20181227j-04-w460

A: Figure 3 shows the number of crime cases in Japan which use ¹(   ) analysis.

B: When its use was started in 1992, there were only ²(   ) cases. By ³(   ), it increased to ⁴(   ), and from 2005, it rose more sharply.

A: Yes, and in 2017, the number was ⁵(   ) cases. This means that it increased ⁶(   ) times from the 1992 figure. That's amazing, isn't it?

B: Yes, it is. Now DNA analysis has become essential in solving crimes.

A: You can say that again! The technology has developed to a level where DNA analysis can identify a particular person out of 4.7 trillion people.

B: Really? That's incredible! So, the police can solve any crimes?

A: Unfortunately, things are not that easy. The police can't completely depend on the ⁷(   ) ⁸(   ) because someone's DNA that remains at the crime scene may be that of someone other than the criminal.

B: Oh, I see. So, traditional investigation methods are still necessary.

NOTES

incredible とても素晴らしい・すごい　investigation 捜査・調査

Discussion

A Agree or disagree?

> **We should continue researching gene-editing on human beings. If we do, then we might be able to prevent people from getting terrible diseases.**

Step 1. <u>Do you agree or disagree with the above idea?</u> Write two or three reasons supporting each side.

Agree

I agree with this idea for the following reasons:

✓ Reason 1

....
....
....
....

✓ Reason 2

....
....
....
....

✓ Reason 3

....
....
....
....

Disagree

I disagree with this idea for the following reasons:

✓ Reason 1

....
....
....
....

✓ Reason 2

....
....
....
....

✓ Reason 3

....
....
....
....

Step 2. | Learn the discussion strategies.

 2-31、32

1. In pairs, read out the following conversation. Write the numbers of the underlined expressions in the appropriate discussion strategies below.

Agreeing _____   Asking for clarification _____

Disagreeing _____   Focusing on one thing _____

• *Example 1:*

> A: ❶I have strong doubts about gene-editing on human beings.

> B: ❷What do you mean by that? Wouldn't it be good to get rid of serious diseases?

> A: ❸I agree on that matter, but that kind of research also might lead to attempts to create an ideal baby, and we don't know what the long-term consequences will be.

• *Example 2:*

> A: I know that there are many kinds of gene-editing experiments that have been carried out on plants and animals, but we have to be more careful and take the right steps ❹when it comes to human beings.

> B: ❺You took the words right out of my mouth. When Japanese academics analyzed the rules on gene-editing in 39 countries in 2014, 29 of those countries, like Canada and Australia, had a legal ban on it.

> A: ❻As far as human beings are concerned, I think we should try to stay on the safe side.

2. In the same conversation, if you find any evidence from an outside source, highlight it.

Step 3. This time, take a different stance from your partner and do a little research. Find more evidence and write a dialogue with your partner.

Step 4. Read the dialogue aloud with your partner.

Step 5. Then, try to come to a conclusion. Whether you come to the same conclusions or not, write the reason why.

Example

- **We reached the same conclusion. Both of us agree with the statement mainly because…**

- **We did not reach the same conclusion. One agrees with the statement mainly because…, and the other disagrees with it mainly because…**

Step 6. Next, form a new group with three other students and have a new discussion about your ideas. You are free to take either side and use any evidence you used in Step 3.

Research Presentation and Writing

Find your own topics for a research presentation or writing related to the unit's theme, or use one of the ones from below:

1. Legal ban on human gene-editing in Japan
2. Changes in people's attitudes towards using gene-editing
3. New businesses using gene-editing in fields other than medical fields

Relationship with Other Countries: Trade War

Introduction

2-33

A Listen to the following news story and fill in the blanks.

In 2018, a trade war between the U.S. and China began. People feared that the global economy would ¹(   ) down because these two countries are the world's two largest economies. The U.S. blamed China for using U.S. intellectual property ²(   ) through American companies operating in China. The U.S. also blamed China for offering too much in ³(   ) on their exporting 5 industries and consequently making the prices of Chinese products much lower than those of other countries. The U.S. ⁴(   ) that these practices were ⁵(   ) in terms of global trade. In order to make China change these practices, the U.S. started to impose high ⁶(   ) on various goods imported from China such as ⁷(   ) and solar panels. China ⁸(   ) by 10 raising the tariffs on U.S. imports such as ⁹(   ) and agricultural products. In this way, both countries tried to damage each other by building huge trade ¹⁰(   ).

B The following are key phrases for the topic. Look them up in your dictionary and write the meanings.

1. the world's two largest economies   _____
2. blame somebody for doing something   _____
3. use intellectual property unlawfully   _____
4. subsidies on exporting industries   _____
5. impose high tariffs on   _____
6. retaliate by doing something   _____

C What do you see in these pictures? Talk about it with your partner.

1.

2.

3.
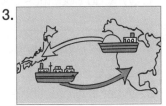

Countries export and import a variety of goods and services. When countries import them, many governments impose tariffs on importers. Tariffs are a tax that the importer has to pay to its own country. It makes it more expensive to import goods and services. As a result, the end price will be higher, and this makes it more
5　expensive for consumers to buy imported items. In this way, governments try to protect their domestic industries. For example, if the price of cheese imported from France is lower than that of domestically produced cheese, this will damage domestic cheese sales. Therefore, the government imposes tariffs on the imported cheese so that the end price for consumers will be more expensive than that of domestic cheese.

10　Because tariffs inhibit trade by raising the price of imported goods, many countries favor free trade. Free trade is conducted when the participating countries agree to ban tariffs under a certain agreement. Some countries make the agreement in their own regional groups such as ASEAN or the EU. The agreements are intended to promote regional economic growth. Others make bilateral agreements, which
15　are agreements between only two countries. One example is an FTA (Free Trade Agreement). Over the years, some FTAs have developed into multilateral agreements like the TPP (Trans-Pacific Partnership).

However, some countries are choosing not to use free trade agreements. They believe that protecting certain domestic industries will be more effective in promoting
20　their own economic growth. This policy is called protectionism. The Trump administration's economic policy is a typical example of this. The administration withdrew from the TPP in 2017, claiming that if goods were imported freely, it would damage domestic industries. It also claims that increasing imports are causing huge trade deficits, which will weaken the country's economic power. The U.K. is also
25　leaving the EU and will limit goods, services and people entering the country from the EU region. This decision to leave is called "Brexit."

A Read the passage and answer the questions.

1. Why do countries impose tariffs?

_____

2. In which ways do countries promote free trade?

_____

3. What is protectionism?

B Complete an outline of the reading passage.

I. How tariffs can protect domestic industries

    A. Tariffs are a _____ imposed on _____.

    B. Tariffs raise the _____.

    C. Consumers have to pay more money to buy the product.

II. Free trade

    A. Tariffs _____ trade by raising the _____ of imported goods.

    B. Many countries favor free trade.

        1. An _____ between participating countries is needed.

        2. The agreement _____ tariffs.

    C. Examples of free trade

        1. Regional

            a. _____ and the _____ are typical examples.

            b. Free trade promotes _____ economic growth.

        2. Bilateral

            a. _____ is an example.

            b. Some FTAs developed into _____ agreements such as _____

III. Protectionism

    A. This is a national _____.

    B. Tariffs work well for a country's _____.

    C. Examples of protectionism

        1. Reasons the Trump administration _____ from TPP

            a. It would _____ domestic industries.

            b. It would cause huge _____.

        2. The U.K. leaves the EU.

            a. This would limit _____, _____ and _____ entering the country.

            b. This is called _____.

Data

A Study the figure and fill in the blanks.

🎧 2-37

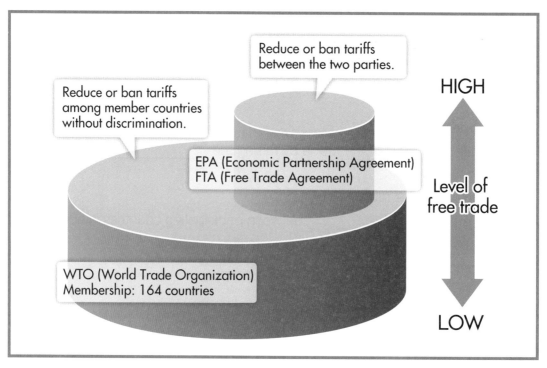

Figure 1: WTO, EPA and FTA

Source: 日本商工会議所 「EPA と FTA や WTO との関係」より作成
https://www.jcci.or.jp/gensanchi/epazenpan.html

Figure 1 shows the relationship of WTO, EPA and FTA. WTO stands for
¹(   ) (   ) (   ). This is the ²(   ) of free
trade. It was established in 1995 and now has as many as ³(   ) countries
as members. These countries cover 98 percent of world trade. One of its policies
5 is to treat all member nations without ⁴(   ). This includes giving
preferential treatment to less developed countries. This means that minimum tariffs
or no tariffs should be imposed on imports from less developed countries. Recently,
more countries have sought a ⁵(   ) level of free trade than allowed by
the WTO. They started to make further agreements individually. These agreements
10 are termed ⁶(   ) and ⁷(   ). There are differences between these
two agreements. The ⁸(   ) aims to ban tariffs mainly on goods, while the
⁹(   ) aims for a wider economic partnership. It not only aims to ban tariffs
but also promotes free exchange in intellectual properties and people, and less
regulation on investments.

NOTES

WTO 世界貿易機関　EPA 経済連携協定　FTA 自由貿易協定
preferential treatment to less developed countries 途上国優遇措置　intellectual properties 知的財産
regulation 規制　investment 投資

112

B Study the table and fill in the blanks.

 2-38

Imported items from the EU	Tariffs before the EPA taking effect	Tariffs after the EPA taking effect
Wine	15% or 125 yen per liter, whichever tariff is lower	Banned immediately
Macaroni, Spaghetti	30 yen per kilogram	Banned after 10 years
Natural cheese	29.8%	Banned after 15 years
Chocolate	10%	Banned after 10 years

Table 1: Japan's tariffs on goods imported from the EU

Source: 税関「実行関税率表（2019 年 2 月 1 日版）第 22 類税率」www.customs.go.jp/tariff/2019_2/data/
j_22.htm および農林水産省「日 EU・EPA における 農林水産物の交渉結果概要① （EU からの輸入）」
www.maff.go.jp/j/kokusai/renkei/fta_kanren/f_eu/attach/pdf/index-53.pdf より作成

A: Did you know that an EPA between Japan and the EU took effect in 2019? This chart shows the change in the tariff rates of some foods [1](   ) from the EU to Japan.

B: Yes, I heard that we can buy goods from Europe much cheaper now than before, but how much cheaper? 5

A: Well, take a look at this chart. The tariff on imported wine was [2](   ) instantly. So in theory, the price of wine will soon drop.

B: That's good news. I noticed that the tariff on [3](   ) (   ) will remain high for a while at 29.8 percent. It will take [4](   ) years to ban it. How come? 10

A: I think that the tariff was originally set high to [5](   ) the domestic cheese industry. It will also take many years for the industry to become competitive enough.

B: I hope the EPA won't damage the production of cheese made in Japan. The same thing can be said for other foods. 15

A: You mean macaroni, spaghetti, and [6](   ) ? Tariffs on imports of these goods from the EU will be banned after [7](   ) years.

B: In the future, we will see more people buying imported foods at supermarkets, I guess.

NOTES

take effect 効力を発する　in theory 理論上　competitive 競争力がある

Discussion

A Agree or disagree?

> **In the future, there should be no barriers in trade. Countries should ban tariffs and promote trade worldwide.**

Step 1. Do you agree or disagree with the above idea? Write two or three reasons supporting each side.

Agree

I agree with this idea for the following reasons:

✓ **Reason 1**

....

....

....

....

✓ **Reason 2**

....

....

....

....

✓ **Reason 3**

....

....

....

....

Disagree

I disagree with this idea for the following reasons:

✓ **Reason 1**

....

....

....

....

✓ **Reason 2**

....

....

....

....

✓ **Reason 3**

....

....

....

....

Step 2. | Learn the discussion strategies. 2-39、49

1. In pairs, read out the following conversation. Write the numbers of the underlined expressions in the appropriate discussion strategies below.

Agreeing ____

Disagreeing ____

Starting a discussion ____

Showing a negative outcome

____

Hypothesizing ____

• *Example 1:*

> **A:** Do you agree that tariffs should be banned to promote trade worldwide?

> **B:** ❶<u>Absolutely</u>, because consumers can buy imported goods cheaper. According to the newspaper, after the EPA between Japan and the EU took effect in 2019, the 15-percent tariff on wine was banned. The price of wine dropped soon after.

> **A:** ❷<u>I think that's a valid point.</u> ❸<u>Having said so, I disagree with this idea</u> because it will seriously damage domestic industries.

• *Example 2:*

> **A:** ❹<u>What's your stance on</u> removing trade barriers between countries?

> **B:** I agree with this idea because ❺<u>without protection, producers would</u> start to find more cost-effective ways to produce their products.

> **A:** ❻<u>That's clearly true.</u> I think competition is a good thing. ❼<u>Otherwise</u>, producers will not try to cut their costs.

2. In the same conversation, if you find any evidence from an outside source, highlight it.

Step 3. This time, take a different stance from your partner and do a little research. Find more evidence and write a dialogue with your partner.

Step 4. Read the dialogue aloud with your partner.

Step 5. Then, try to come to a conclusion. Whether you come to the same conclusions or not, write the reason why.

Example

• **We reached the same conclusion. Both of us agree with the statement mainly because···**

• **We did not reach the same conclusion. One agrees with the statement mainly because···, and the other disagrees with it mainly because···**

Step 6. Next, form a new group with three other students and have a new discussion about your ideas. You are free to take either side and use any evidence you used in Step 3.

Research Presentation and Writing

Find your own topics for a research presentation or writing related to the unit's theme, or use one of the ones from below:

1. Preferential treatment by the WTO
2. TPP without the US
3. Protecting intellectual property

UNIT 14

Religions: Changes in Islam

Introduction

🔊 2-41

A **Listen to the following news story and fill in the blanks.**

In June, 2018, a ban on women driving ended in ¹( ). It was
the only country in the world where women were ²( ) from driving
because Saudi Arabia follows a ³( ) form of Sunni Islam. The lifting of the
ban is part of Crown Prince's program to ⁴( ) Saudi society. Around
the same time, women were allowed to attend a ⁵( ) game at a stadium 5
in ⁶( ) after 40 years of being banned, though they were separated from
the male soccer fans by a ⁷( ). The government believed if women and
men sit together, it could lead to ⁸( ) society's morals. FIFA, the
international governing body of world soccer, however, persuaded Iran to allow
women to attend games to promote gender ⁹( ).   10

B **The following are key phrases for the topic. Look them up in your**
dictionary and write the meanings.

1. A ban on driving is   _____
2. The ban was ended/ lifted/ ended   _____
3. modernize society   _____
4. follow Islam   _____
5. limit women's freedom   _____

C **What do you see in these pictures? Talk about it with your partner.**

1.  2.  3.

117

Islam is a religion founded by the Prophet Muhammad and based on a holy book called the Koran. Muhammad was born in 570 A.D. in Mecca in Saudi Arabia and delivered messages from Allah, the Muslim word for God. Islam has five requirements, called the Five Pillars of Islam. Believers are required to believe in one God, pray
5　five times a day, give money or services to the poor, spend a period of time without eating or drinking, and visit Mecca once in their lifetime. Recently in Islamic society, three major points have slowly changed: women's dress codes, gender separation rules, and conflicts between Sunni and Shia.

Dress codes and gender separation rules have limited women's freedom. It is
10　said that those customs were originally Persian or Byzantine-Christian, and Muslims adopted them in the 7th century. Recently, however, some Muslim women have stopped wearing garments that cover their entire body, and have started to play a more active role in society, although most still wear a headscarf called a "hijab." Those women follow the Koran's teaching to dress modestly. Also, in traditional
15　Muslim societies, women usually kept to their roles of homemaking and childcare, but because of recent changes Muslim women are becoming more educated and working in careers such as law and medicine.

The division of Islam into Sunni and Shia has caused a lot of political conflicts, but some people are working to help the two sides accept each other. Ninety percent
20　of Muslims are Sunnis, and the remaining ten percent are Shias. The dispute between them was originally over who should be considered Muhammad's legitimate successor. A 2017 survey of 4,000 young people in Egypt reported that 80 percent wished to end the conflicts between the two groups. In Lebanon, thanks to an NGO, people in the two sects have been restoring roads and buildings together since 2018.
25　In Oman, they have even held religious services together.

A **Read the passage and answer the questions.**

1. Name the "Five Pillars of Islam."

_____

2. Describe the changes in women's dress codes and gender separation in Muslim society.

_____

3. What has been happening lately between the Sunni and Shia sects?

B Complete an outline of the reading passage.

I. What is Islam?

    A. As a religion

        1. Based on a holy book called the _____.

        2. _____ delivered messages from Allah.

        3. The five _____ are called the Five Pillars of Islam.

    B. Recent changes include three main points:

        1. Women's dress codes

        2. _____ rules

        3. Conflicts between two sects - _____

II. Changes in women's dress codes and gender separation rules

    A. Some women stopped _____ that cover their entire bodies.

    B. More women are becoming more educated and working in careers such as ___ and _____.

III. Changes in conflict between Sunnis and Shias

    A. Some people are working to help them accept each other.

    B. A survey shows _____ of 4,000 young people in Egypt wished to ____ _____.

    C. An NGO helped people in the two sects to restore roads and buildings _____ in Lebanon.

    D. People in the two sects have held _____ together in Oman.

Data

A Study the figures and fill in the blanks.

 2-45

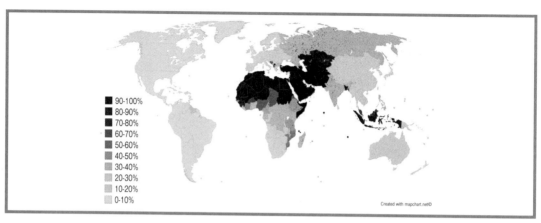

Figure 1: Muslim Population in 2014

Source: Pew Research Center, "World Muslim population by percentage (2018 Estimate)" より作成
https://en.wikipedia.org/wiki/Islam_by_country

Figure 1 shows the percentage of Muslims in each country. Most countries in the ¹( ) and North ²( ) follow Islam. Additionally,
5 in Asia, ³( ) also has a high percentage of Muslims. In fact, it has the world's largest Muslim population, with about 200 million living there. Other countries such as Pakistan, Afghanistan,
10 Turkmenistan, and Uzbekistan are also Islamic countries. India falls into the ⁴( ) range, but it has the second largest Muslim population after Indonesia. This is because there are 1.3
15 billion people living in India.

Figure 2: Estimated distribution of Sunni Muslims in the Middle East

Source: BBC News "Sunnis and Shia in the Middle East." Data from CRS, Pew Research, CIA world factbook " Estimated distribution of Sunni Muslims in the Middle East" より作成
https://www.bbc.com/news/world-middle-east-25434060

Figure 2 shows the estimated distribution of ⁵( ) Muslims in the Middle East. More than 80 percent of people in Saudi Arabia and ⁶( ) follow Sunni teachings. Syria, Jordan, and the ⁷( ) have a higher
20 percentage as well. In contrast, ⁸( ) and Oman have a lower percentage. That means a lot of their population are ⁹( ) Muslims. Conflict between them is sometimes caused by competition for economic and political dominance, rather than differences in religious teachings and practices.

fall into 分類される   estimated distribution 予測(推定)分布   dominance 支配・優位

B Study the figures and fill in the blanks.

 2-46

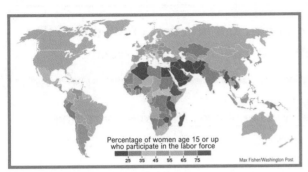

Percentage of women age 15 or up who participate in the labor force

25   35   45   55   65   75

Max Fisher/Washington Post

Figure 3: The percentage of women who participate in the labor force

Source: Max Fisher in The Washington Post "Where women work, and don't: A map of female labor force participation around the world" in 2014. Data from World Bank / World Development Indicators. https://www.washingtonpost.com/news/worldviews/wp/2014/02/13/where-women-work-and-dont-a-map-of-female-labor-force-participation-around-the-world/?noredirect=on

A: Figure 3 shows the percentage of women in the labor force. You can see that Yemen, [1]( ), Iraq, and [2]( ) in the Middle East, and Egypt and [3]( ) in North Africa belong to the red zones.

B: That means the ratio is only [4]( ) percent at most. That's a low figure.

A: Yes, Muslims adopted a custom that women were

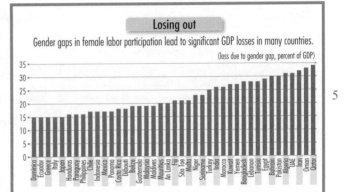

Losing out

Gender gaps in female labor participation lead to significant GDP losses in many countries.

(loss due to gender gap, percent of GDP)

Figure 4: Gender gaps in female participation lead to GDP losses.

Source: IMF STAFF DISCUSSION NOTE "Fail Play: More Equal Laws Boost Female Labor Force Participation"

https://www.imf.org/external/pubs/ft/sdn/2015/sdn1502.pdf

separated from men with curtains and walls. In addition, men and women had a clear distinction of their roles, and only men dealt with the outside world.

B: It seems that women are taken good care of by men in their culture, but in modern society, women don't seem to have as much freedom or the same rights as men.

A: Yes, that's true. Also, women can be an important labor force in the economy. As you can see in Figure 4, it is obvious that when women do not participate in the labor force, it leads to [5]( ) losses.

B: And in this graph, the worst losses take place in the Middle East and [6]( ). They lose about [7]( ) percent of their GDP.

A: The Brookings Institution in America calculates if women worked as much as men, the GDP would increase about 47 percent in 10 years in this region.

NOTES

labor force 労働力   losing out 損をする(取りそこなう)   gender gaps 男女差   GDP 国内総生産

Discussion

A Agree or disagree?

> **We should change some of the teachings and practices of religion so that they are more in tune with the life and values of modern society.**

Step 1. Do you agree or disagree with the above idea? Write two or three reasons supporting each side.

Agree

> *I agree with this idea for the following reasons.*

✓ Reason 1

....
....
....
....

✓ Reason 2

....
....
....
....

✓ Reason 3

....
....
....
....

Disagree

> *I disagree with this idea for the following reasons.*

✓ Reason 1

....
....
....
....

✓ Reason 2

....
....
....
....

✓ Reason 3

....
....
....
....

2-47、48

Step 2. Learn the discussion strategies.

1. In pairs, read out the following conversation. Write the numbers of the underlined expressions in the appropriate discussion strategies below.

Agreeing ____

Disagreeing ____

Giving your opinion ____

Asking for more explanation ____

Referring to a source ____

Hesitating ____

Saying in different words ____

• *Example 1:*

A: ❶In my view, we should change some teachings and practices.

B: I agree because religious believers are living in the modern age.

A: That's true. In other words, they can't live without making changes.

B: ❷I have no objection to this idea. Especially, ❸as the International Monetary Fund (IMF) reported, if women participated in the labor force, it would bring a lot of benefits to a country.

• *Example 2:*

A: ❹I oppose changing some teachings and practices because it might change the original beliefs of the religion. Religion is one aspect of culture and contains unique values.

B: ❺Can you explain what culture is? I thought that culture would change with the times because culture reflects our behavior and values.

A: ❻Well, ❼what I mean is that we should pass our own ideas to future generations.

2. In the same conversation, if you find any evidence from an outside source, highlight it.

Step 3. This time, take a different stance from your partner and do a little research. Find more evidence and write a dialogue with your partner.

Step 4. Read the dialogue aloud with your partner.

Step 5. Then, try to come to a conclusion. Whether you come to the same conclusions or not, write the reason why.

Example

- **We reached the same conclusion. Both of us agree with the statement mainly because…**

- **We did not reach the same conclusion. One agrees with the statement mainly because…, and the other disagrees with it mainly because…**

Step 6. Next, form a new group with three other students and have a new discussion about your ideas. You are free to take either side and use any evidence you used in Step 3.

Research Presentation and Writing

Find your own topics for a research presentation or writing related to the unit's theme, or use one of the ones from below:

1. Reactions to some changes in Islam
2. Research on a major conflict between Sunnis and Shias
3. Problems and changes in other religions

Right to Be Forgotten: Privacy and Freedom of Expression

Introduction

2-49

A Listen to the following news story and fill in the blanks.

A Japanese man filed a lawsuit seeking to have his ¹( ) record for child prostitution removed from Google's search results. He said that continuing to display the ²( ) violated his personal rights. The Saitama District Court accepted his argument in 2015, but the Tokyo High Court overturned it in 2016. In January, 2017, Japan's Supreme Court also ³( ) his demand, 5 ruling that to do so would violate freedom of ⁴( ). The court said that the removal of search engine results can be allowed only when the protection of ⁵( ) is more important than giving the information to the ⁶( ).

B The following are key phrases for the topic. Look them up in your dictionary and write the meanings.

1. Google search results _____
2. ask search engines to remove links _____
3. information disclosure _____
4. against the law _____
5. posted on the Internet _____
6. relevant to society _____
7. public interest _____

C What do you see in these pictures? Talk about it with your partner.

1.
2.
3.

FREEDOM

The Right to be Forgotten is the right to request that personal information be removed from the Internet. In 2011, a French woman requested that nude photos of her be removed from Google search results and it was accepted. This led to the introduction of this regulation in the European Union in 2012. It says individuals
5 have the right to ask search engines to remove links with personal data under certain conditions. It enables people to control their personal data because such data can have a negative impact on their privacy. In other words, their reputation might be damaged if such data is left on the Internet.

The regulation outlines the circumstances under which the right applies. It says
10 the right applies if the information disclosure is against the law. Such examples include child pornography and information that might lead to criminal conduct. The right would also cover embarrassing content posted on the Internet without consent, such as revenge porn. The regulation also says that the right applies if the data is out of date or inaccurate. In addition, if the data is no longer relevant to society, it is more
15 likely to be removed. For example, news about someone's divorce is less important than news about crimes.

Google has received a lot of removal requests, and many of them relate to people's professional lives. For example, doctors who were accused of malpractice want to have that information removed, but this may be of interest to people who are
20 searching for a good doctor. Another example is about government officials who want to have their prior political views removed if they have changed them. However, there is public interest in accessing those past views. Google said the removal should be an exception and should only occur when there is a legitimate reason. It said a search engine should not be in a position to decide whether contents should be
25 removed or not.

A Read the passage and answer the questions.

1. What is the Right to Be Forgotten?

_____

2. Under what circumstances does the right apply?

_____

3. What do many of the removal requests relate to?

_____

B Complete an outline of the reading passage.

I. The right to be forgotten

    A. Requesting _____ be removed

        1. Personal information is removed from _____.

        2. Individuals ask search engines to remove _____.

    B. Controlling _____

        1. Data can have a negative impact on _____.

        2. Someone's _____ might be damaged.

II. Circumstances under which the right applies

    A. Information _____ is against the law.

    B. _____ content is posted without _____.

    C. The data is out of date or _____.

    D. The data is no longer _____ to the society.

III. Google's policy

    A. Requests received

        1. There were a lot of _____.

        2. Many of the requests relate to people's _____.

    B. Removal conditions

        1. It should be an _____.

        2. There should be a _____ reason.

        3. Search engines should not decide on the _____.

Data

A Study the figure and fill in the blanks. 2-53

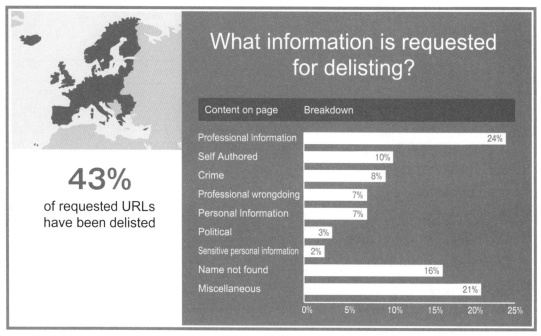

43%
of requested URLs
have been delisted

Figure 1: The Right to be Forgotten, Summary of requests from 2014-2017

Source: google "Updating our right to be forgotten Transparency Report"
https://www.blog.google/around-the-globe/google-europe/updating-our-right-be-forgotten-transparency-report/

Figure 1 shows a summary of delisting ¹(　　　　　　) in Europe from 2014 to ²(　　　　). It was released by Google in its Transparency Report. According to the data, ³(　　　) percent of requested URLs have been delisted from Google Search and the rest of the requests have been rejected. The figure shows some of the URLs that have been delisted. As shown in the bar graph, the delisted
5 content is classified into ⁴(　　　　) categories. About one-fourth of the content is ⁵(　　　　　　) (　　　　　　) such as a work address and phone number. ⁶(　　　　), for example, information about the victim, makes up 8 percent. Professional wrongdoing, such as bribery and corruption, makes up 7 percent.
10 Personal information, such as images or videos of an individual, also makes up ⁷(　　) percent.

NOTES

delist ～を除く　Transparency Report 透明性レポート

B Study the figure and fill in the blanks.

 2-54

A: In Figure 2, you see a scale that shows freedom of expression is more important than privacy. Japan's Supreme Court sets six factors when removing search engine results. The ¹( ) of the information is the first factor.

B: What content is least likely to be removed?

A: Information about politicians' speeches is less likely to be removed because it is important for the public when they decide who to vote for.

B: I see. What is the second factor?

A: The degree of ²( ) caused to privacy is the second factor.

B: Can you give an example?

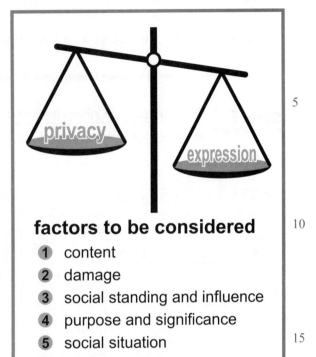

factors to be considered

1. content
2. damage
3. social standing and influence
4. purpose and significance
5. social situation
6. necessity of reporting

Figure 2: The Right to be Forgotten, Factors to be considered

Source: 忘れられる権利（Wikipedia）より作成
https://ja.wikipedia.org/ 忘れられる権利

A: If only a limited number of people can access the information, the damage will be limited. Therefore, this kind of information doesn't have to be removed. For example, people who don't know the specific words for the search, such as the person's name or where he or she lives, will not be able to access the information.

B: The third factor is social ³( ) and influence.

A: For example, doctors are important in society and have a great influence on the public, so information about medical malpractice is less likely to be removed.

B: The other factors are ⁴( ) and significance, social ⁵( ), and ⁶( ) of reporting.

A: This means, for example, crime is a great concern for the public, so reporting it has social significance. Therefore, that kind of information will not be removed.

NOTES

freedom of expression 表現の自由　medical malpractice 医療過誤

Discussion

A Agree or disagree?

> **The Right to Be Forgotten is more important than freedom of expression.**

Step 1. Do you agree or disagree with the above idea? Write two or three reasons supporting each side.

Agree	Disagree
I agree with this idea because of the following reasons.	*I disagree with this idea because of the following reasons.*

Agree

I agree with this idea because of the following reasons.

✓ Reason 1

....
....
....
....

✓ Reason 2

....
....
....
....

✓ Reason 3

....
....
....
....

Disagree

I disagree with this idea because of the following reasons.

✓ Reason 1

....
....
....
....

✓ Reason 2

....
....
....
....

✓ Reason 3

....
....
....
....

Step 2. Learn the discussion strategies. 2-55、56

1. In pairs, read out the following conversation. Write the numbers of the underlined expressions in the appropriate discussion strategies below.

Referring to a source ____   **Asking for an opinion** ____

Agreeing ____   **Disagreeing** ____

Giving your opinion ____

• *Example 1:*

A: ❶So, what's your opinion about the Right to Be Forgotten? Do you think it is more important than freedom of expression?

B: I think so. If my private photos were posted on the Internet, it would be embarrassing.

A: ❷That's exactly what I was going to say. ❸The National Police Agency reported that in 2018, Japan continued to see more than 1,000 cases of embarrassing photos posted on the Internet. I think measures should be taken to prevent that.

• *Example 2:*

A: Today, we're going to discuss the Right to Be Forgotten.

B: ❹I'm quite sure that it's a good idea because privacy is important.

A: ❺I don't think that's a good idea because we have the right to know. Experts say people should have the right to access information, and preservation of historical, scientific, and statistical data is important.

2. In the same conversation, if you find any evidence from an outside source, highlight it.

Step 3. This time, take a different stance from your partner and do a little research. Find more evidence and write a dialogue with your partner.

Step 4. Read the dialogue aloud with your partner.

Step 5. Then, try to come to a conclusion. Whether you come to the same conclusions or not, write the reason why.

Example

- **We reached the same conclusion. Both of us agree with the statement mainly because⋯**

- **We did not reach the same conclusion. One agrees with the statement mainly because⋯, and the other disagrees with it mainly because⋯**

Step 6. Next, form a new group with three other students and have a new discussion about your ideas. You are free to take either side and use any evidence you used in Step 3.

Research Presentation and Writing

Find your own topics for a research presentation or writing related to the unit's theme, or use one of the ones from below:

1. Press freedom and censorship
2. Social media and the protection of personal information
3. Freedom of speech in Japan and the Designated Secrets Law

Discussion Dialogue

Statement			
Speakers		Date	

	Dialogue		
Speaker 1	I agree with this idea because		
	Evidence:		
	Source:		
Speaker 2			
	Evidence:		
	Source:		
Speaker 1			
	Evidence:		
	Source:		
Speaker 2			
	Evidence:		
	Source:		

Useful expressions

- **Starting a discussion**

Today, we're going to discuss…

What do you think about this topic (this idea)?

Today's topic is…

- **Giving your opinion**

I think that… because…   I feel/believe/ suppose…

I personally think…

In my opinion…   I'd like to say (that)…   May I say (that)…

Can I answer that?   Can I respond to that?

In my view…

As far as I can tell…   I'm pretty

My opinion is that…   Honestly speaking,…   I would say…

- **Responding to others**

I see.   I understand.   Really?   Yeah.   Is that right?

Well,…   Um,…

- **Saying in different words**

What I mean is…   Let me put it this way.

Let me rephrase that.   Let me put it into other words.

In other words,…   That is…

- **Agreeing**

I agree.   That's a good point.   That's a great idea.

I totally agree with you.

(I think) you're right.   That's right.   I think so, too.

Me too.

Exactly.   I agree entirely.   I feel the same way.

I see what you mean.

Absolutely.   I didn't think of that!   That's just what I thought.

I agree with you on that matter.   You can say that again.

Definitely.   That's exactly what I was going to say.

You took the words right out of my mouth.

You've got that right.   I'm completely convinced.   I support that idea.

There are no objections.   I have no objection to that idea.

That makes sense.

That's clearly true.   That's a valid point.

I'm definitely with you.

• Disagreeing

That's a good point, but⋯   I'm afraid I disagree.

Actually, I think⋯   I don't think so.   Sorry, but⋯

I don't think that's a good idea because⋯   Maybe, but⋯

That may be true, but⋯   I don't agree with your thinking.

I guess so, but⋯   I see what you mean, but I'm against it.

I have a different opinion.   I'm not sure I agree because⋯

You have a point there, but⋯   It's interesting, but I found something different.

That may be true, but I'm opposed to it.   I oppose the idea that⋯

I disagree with you on most you said.   ⋯but even so, my stance is the opposite

That's one way of looking at it, but⋯

To a certain extent, yes, but⋯

Are you sure? Actually, I learned that most people⋯

I'm firmly opposed to this decision.

Having said so, I think⋯   I have strong doubts about this idea.

• Asking for an opinion

What do you think?   What's your opinion?   How about you?

What do you think about it?   Could I have your opinion?

Do you agree?   Don't you think it is a good idea?

What's your stance on this idea?

• Asking for clarification

Excuse me?   Pardon?   Did you say…?   Could you repeat it?

Sorry?   I don't understand.   What do you mean?   What did you say?

You mean…?   In other words, …?   I think you said…, right?

What was the first point?   I'm not sure I understand.

Sorry, could you say that again, please?   Could you repeat that for me, please?

Would you mind repeating that?   Could you repeat it more slowly?

What exactly does that mean?   What do you mean by that?

Could you explain this word, please?   Can you tell me what it means?

I'm sorry, I couldn't hear what you said.   I didn't quite catch what you said.

I'm afraid you've lost me.   Sorry, I didn't quite follow what you were saying.

• Showing importance

The key is…

What I want to say is…   What I mean is…

The important thing here is that…

• Listing points

The first point is…   To begin with, …   Secondly, …

Lastly, …

Finally, …

• Giving another point

What do you think about the other case?   What about Japan?

• Giving a cause and effect

···because···   ···, so···

Because of···   Due to···   As a result, ···

A results from B.   A results in B.   A leads to B.

Therefore···   Consequently···

• Checking understanding

Do you understand what I mean?   Do you follow me?

Are you with me?   Do you know what I mean?

• Hesitating

Well···   Let me see/ think.

How shall I put it?   How can I say it?

I'm not sure how to ask you this···   Um, ···

• Not sure

I guess.   I suppose so.   Actually, I don't know.

I'm not really sure about that.

I haven't made up my mind yet.   It's hard to say.

• Comparing and contrasting

Also,···   is / are like ···   ···, but···   ··· while

Likewise, ···   A is different from B.

A is the same as B.

Similarly, ···   A is similar to B.   In contrast, ···

On the other hand, ···

In the past, it was···, but the situation is different now.

- **Interrupting someone**

Excuse me, but could I ask something?   Excuse me, but I have a question.
Sorry for interrupting, but···

- **Asking for more explanations**

Could you give me an example?   I'd like to know more about···
Could you tell me why?
Could you be more specific?
How does *A* affect *B*?   Can you explain the relationship between *A* and *B*?
Can you tell me more?

- **Showing examples**

In cases such as···,   Take ··· as an example.
For example /instance,

- **Asking for help**

Could someone/ you help me explain that?

- **Referring to a source**

I read that···   I heard that···
According to the newspaper, ···   According to an article I read, …
The newspaper/article said/ showed/ reported/ that···
Prof. A suggests/ explains/ reports/ states/ maintains/ argues that···
A research conducted in 2018 by the United Nations shows that···
The data is based on···   As the article shows, ···

- **Explaining the problem**

There are two problems. One is···/ The other is ···

- **Giving a solution**

The problem will be solved by⋯   Probably the best thing to do is⋯

- **Hypothesizing**

If that kind of incident happened, we would not be able to⋯
If *A* is to do *B*, they should do *C*.
Imagine how something will be if⋯
It must be⋯

- **Reaching a decision**

Right. So, do we agree?
In the end, I think that is the best option.
Good, so our final decision is⋯ / We all agree with that statement.

- **Showing a negative outcome**

Otherwise, ⋯

- **Adding ideas**

On top of that, ⋯   In addition, ⋯   Besides that, ⋯

- **Showing a positive/negative point**

The good/bad thing is that⋯
The advantage/disadvantage of *A* is that⋯
⋯have a great advantage/disadvantage.

- **Focusing on one topic**

When it comes to this point, ⋯   Regarding this point, ⋯
On that matter, ⋯   As far as this point is concerned, ⋯

For Discussion Facilitators

1. Today, we're going to discuss _____.
     Or
   Today's topic is _____.

2. There must be pros and cons, but I think that
   _____.

3. What do you think about it, Mr. (Miss) _____.?
     Or
   Do you agree with me, or not, Mr. (Miss)
   _____.?

4. How about Mr. (Miss)   ? What do you think about it?

5. Do you have any other opinions?

6. We reached the same conclusion. We agree with the statement
   mainly because... .
        Or
   We did not reach the same conclusion. (Two students) agree with
   the statement mainly because... , and the others disagree with it
   mainly because... .

7. Today, we discussed _____.

8. That's it for today. Thank you for your cooperation.

TEXT PRODUCTION STAFF

edited by 編集
Eiichi Tamura 田村 栄一

cover design by 表紙デザイン
Nobuyoshi Fujino 藤野 伸芳

text design by 本文デザイン
Hiroyuki Kinouchi (ALIUS) 木野内 宏行 (アリウス)

illustrated by イラスト
Yoko Sekine 関根 庸子
Kyosuke Kuromaru 黒丸 恭介

CD PRODUCTION STAFF

narrated by 吹き込み者
Howard Colefield (AmerE) ハワード・コールフィールド (アメリカ英語)
Jennifer Okano (AmerE) ジェニファー・オカノ (アメリカ英語)

CLIL : Discuss the Changing World
CLIL：英語で考える現代社会

2020年1月20日 初版 発行
2023年2月25日 第5刷 発行

著　者　仲谷 都　油木田 美由紀
　　　　山崎 勝　Chad L. Godfrey

発行者　佐野 英一郎
発行所　株式会社 成美堂
　　　　〒101-0052　東京都千代田区神田小川町3-22
　　　　TEL 03-3291-2261　FAX 03-3293-5490
　　　　https://www.seibido.co.jp

印刷・製本　倉敷印刷 (株)

ISBN 978-4-7919-7208-1　　　　　　　　Printed in Japan